Morris Telford's Salopian Odyssey

By Russell Payne

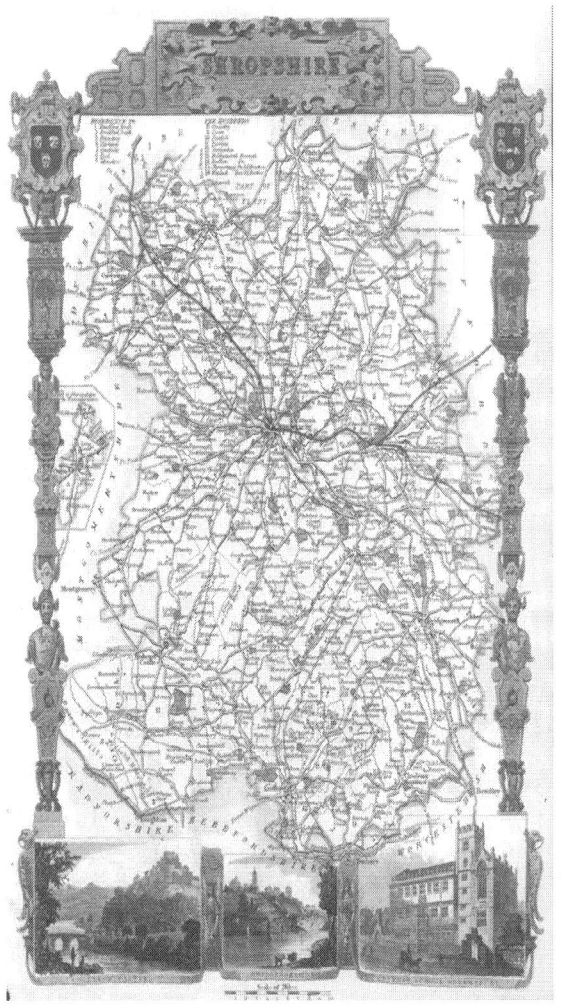

Morris Telford's Salopian Odyssey

This edition Published 2010 by Lulu

© Russell Payne, 2004

A Rabid Antelope product

http://www.rabid.oneuk.com

Cover Design by Ray Bid

Back cover photos –

"Hong Kong Bingo" – taken by Stewart Knight

"Morris pointing" – taken by Wendy Payne

ISBN 978-1-4457-1726-5

For Wend

The planets prettiest proofreader

WEEK 1 DAY 1

I made a decision today - I'm going to change the world. My name is Morris Telford, though I do not have the good fortune to reside in the shining towers of Telford, instead I live in Moreton Say.

I work in a small office and I am responsible for consumables and procurement, I order the paperclips.

I live with my Mother and her sister, not because of any inability to live alone or form a lasting relationship with a woman, but due to a shrewd financial plan.

I have been saving money since 1989 and today I am going to quit my job, pack my bag, or possibly bags, and go out there, beyond Moreton Say, beyond Telford, beyond even Oswestry to make my mark on the world, to right wrongs, to expose the hidden conspiracies, to damp the fires of evil with my hose of truth.

I intend to travel the world in these times of discontent and violence, meet new and interesting people and tell them about Shropshire and how they should visit it.

First thing this morning, over breakfast, broke the news to my Mother and Aunt Felicity.

There was much wailing, recriminations, shouting, spilling of milk and weeping but after I calmed down it still seemed the correct course of action.

First I need to quit my job, I am setting off now to say farewell forever to office consumables. Wish me luck.

WEEK 1 DAY 2

Yesterday I strode into my manager's office, an overbearing little Hitler called Mr Magson, blazing with pride and determination. I had prepared a written speech-

"Mr Magson, I come to you today not to discuss the ordering of office consumables or petty problems with procurement, I come to speak my mind. I have given this company the best years of my life, while others fulfilled their dreams, stayed up until late at parties and suchlike, my dreams were about responsibility and ordering paperclips, toner, packs of A4 copier paper. You have tried to stifle me, wear me down, bully me into submission over the years, it ends right here. Listen to me now, no more shall my life be ruled by your blinkered little autocracy, I quit, I hand in my notice, I tell you to take your job and shove it. You shall not see me or my like again, I am leaving and will not return."

I spent ages writing that.

So I walked into his office yesterday and Mr Magson is on three weeks holiday in Goa. I left him a note.

I said goodbye to those in the office who had been kind to me. Theresa who bought me Jammie Dodgers and Greta from accounts who looked like an even older Charlie Dimmock.

As a final stroke of defiance to his regime, before I left I over ordered the laser printer toner cartridges, they now have enough to last until December 2008 by which time that model of printer will almost certainly be obsolete. Justice has been served.

I spent today packing, tonight is my last night at home, my mind is made up. Mother is sceptical; she seems to think she can measure the time period I intend to stay away for by counting the clean underwear I take with me. I explained that most 33-year-old men leave their Mothers much earlier and she must accept I am going for good. She just smiled and returned to counting my Y-fronts.

I owe a lot to my parents, especially my Father and Mother, but now I am at a crossroads and need to take the less travelled route – in this case the A41 southbound.

Tomorrow my new life begins.

WEEK 1 DAY 3

AM - So this is it.

I'm officially leaving home. Saying goodbye to over thirty years of my memories, farewell to my room, au revoir to my haven of cloying love. My mother is crying so I will update this later.

I'm going to change the world by searching out injustice instead of turning away from it, by putting things right instead of leaving them be and by learning, understanding and acceptance instead of ignorance, fear and hatred.

PM - I am in an electrical retailers in the thriving metropolis of Market Drayton trying out some palmtop PCs that I can update this blog with as I live my life. I want to be able to write on the move, plucking the essence of the moment from the immediate vibe. The shop assistant is reading this and he (his badge says Gavin) wants to know what my blog is about. Well, Gavin, it's about life, about my personal struggle to make a difference. He's taking the palmt

HI IM GAVIN –

Gavin has been very helpful. I'm going to buy this model and catch a bus.

LATER PM - Met a girl on the bus, she didn't give her name but she was lovely, she looked like a younger Emma Freud. I told her I was from Moreton Say and wanted to change the world. She asked me how but her stop came before I could think of a good answer.

After she got off I thought of some really good answers. I would have said I'm going to change the world by searching out injustice instead of turning away from it, by putting things right instead of leaving them be and by learning, understanding and acceptance instead of ignorance, fear and hatred. Sort of a cross between Batman and Jesus.

WEEK 1 DAY 4

Stayed in a modest B&B just outside Shrewsbury. Had a fried breakfast that looked spectacular but had no discernible flavour.

I started talking to an elderly couple (Richard and Kay) from Kent over breakfast. I asked them what world problems they would like to see addressed. I expected an answer like world famine, or Iraq, or terrorism, or immigration, or disease, instead they both agreed that the world problem that most desperately need addressing was the uneven pavements around where they live in Kent, and proceeded to tell me in great detail how Kay nearly had a nasty fall last Tuesday. Just goes to show that perspective is everything.

I've put 'pavements in Kent' on my list of wrongs to right. Not a high priority, but it's there.

WEEK 1 DAY 5

I walked around Shrewsbury today, talked to as many people as possible.

It's hard to make casual conversation with strangers here.

In Moreton Say I can talk to anyone and expect a conversation, in Shrewsbury most of the people I approach either accuse me of trying to sell them something, tell me to go away or run off themselves, sometimes all three.

One person I did talk to today was Toby. Toby is 18, homeless and was squatting in a doorway with a smile and a polystyrene cup, asking for money. I sat with him for a while and saw all the people avoid eye contact, some stopped and gave him some cash, but no-one seemed to want to talk to him. He told me he 'didn't get on' with his parents and left home at 16, had a bedsit for a few months then ran out of money. Seemed like a nice, positive young man.

I told Toby about Moreton Say and gave him my mother's address and some busfare. She has a spare room.

WEEK 1 DAY 6

I went to a fast food outlet for dinner today. I've seen them advertised on TV but I've never actually been to one before and was strangely excited at the prospect of a branded burger.

It was massively disappointing. Everyone in the queue seemed to be late for something and on a mobile phone. The staff all looked ill and their smiles had a tortured, vacant, drug-induced look to them. A couple of young female staff seemed to be suffering from nervous exhaustion, holding onto the counter to stay upright, but still smiling that desperate smile. Their eyes were not smiling, their eyes were crying out for help.

I ordered a burger and fries, they looked much better on the back-lit menu photo than they did in person.

After eating, I asked to see the manager. When he arrived his name was Robin and he appeared to be 12, possibly 13 years of age. He asked me what I wanted and when I explained I was worried about his staff, they seemed under pressure and stressed, Robin seemed to lose interest. He asked me if I had a specific complaint and again I said yes, I do have a complaint, your staff seem under pressure and stressed. He didn't take me seriously and was very dismissive, so I told him I was from head office and he was to close the restaurant right now.

He didn't believe me so I left while he was checking with head office. I tried to get some of the staff to come with me, quit there and then and find a better life, but they told me, in the coarsest terms, to go away.

WEEK 1 DAY 7

Feeling a bit disheartened today, so I watched some daytime TV in my room and slipped from disheartened to losing the will to breathe.

I feel like I've failed already. I haven't really thought through this whole changing the world thing. Yesterday I was faced with miserable people working in miserable conditions and couldn't do anything about it, worse still the restaurant was full of people oblivious to the suffering of the staff serving them.

I want to alter the world consciousness for the better, make people see how much nicer things would be if they just took an interest in one another. How can I do that if I can't even cheer up some staff at a fast-food chain?

I need a plan.

WEEK 2 DAY 1

Sleepless night last night, I miss the familiar comforts of home, the delicate haven of my old bedroom, my Star Wars duvet cover, my collection of bingo markers and the close proximity of Sophia.

Sophia lived next door and resembled Felicity Kendal, only younger. I never had the courage to ask her out, actually I never had the courage to speak to her, though I did once clean her guttering.

That isn't a euphemism for anything. Her guttering was clogged. It needed cleaning. I cleaned it.

I waited until she was out though.

The first week of my personal odyssey hasn't really gone as well as I had expected - no front-page headlines, no outstanding triumphs. I'm beginning to realise that good intentions and 13 years saving money are not in themselves enough to change the world.

It takes more than that; I need not only to be a man of compassion but a man of action.

In saying that, I have managed to travel further from home than ever before, nearly 80 miles so far. I need to apply myself to having a greater impact on the world.

Not in a devastating impact way like a meteor hitting the earth and wiping out millions of lives, more a general surprise to everyone, like when Will Young won Pop Idol.

To make a modest start I visited the Job Centre today and compiled a list of alternative occupational opportunities that might appeal to someone disillusioned with the fast-food service industry and from these made up a number of 'job-packs' by utilising the photocopying facilities at a nearby library.

I just need to think of a way to distribute these packs to those poor people I saw at that restaurant.

WEEK 2 DAY 2

AM - All the television seems to talk about at the moment is situation with Iraq.

I've considered travelling to see Saddam Hussein and see if I can't sort things out but when I called Lunn Poly they told me travel to Iraq is not currently a package they offer.

So I've decided on a preliminary plan - to contact Tony Blair, (and then possibly his friend George Bush) and explain how easy things could be if we all just try to get along with each other.

I feel that a personal visit from someone who understands the inner workings of a happy community can offer some useful pointers, if Tony realises that what happens in the global village can be just as happy as the village of Moreton Say in Shropshire, then we can put an end to all this talk of war before the missiles start flying around.

I mean, what if one of them misses London? It could hit Shropshire.

PM - I tried to get hold of Tony, he seems to be avoiding me.

I did speak to a number of the staff at Downing Street where Tony lives and finally got through to a man called Gregory who sounded very important.

I explained at length my goal of a socio-political system based on Shropshire village life, specifically Moreton Say and how important it is that people just try and get on with each other.

He promised to pass the message on to Tony as soon as he saw him. Gregory also told me not to bother calling George Bush as he was sure Tony would tell George all about me.

So that's world peace sorted and war averted. Not a bad day's work.

WEEK 2 DAY 3

Fresh with enthusiasm from sharing my vision with Gregory yesterday, I decided to revisit the fast-food restaurant, scene of my previous disillusionments.

I ordered a vanload of sandwiches and pastries from a local bakery and had them deliver to the front of the restaurant and park outside.

I fashioned a sign offering free food to anyone considering eating inside the fast-food restaurant and waited for the place to empty.

Then I entered the restaurant, a beacon of new hope for the grill chefs, a glowing messiah of opportunity for the service assistants, and started handing out the job-packs I had prepared to the otherwise unoccupied staff.

I also offered a cash incentive to anyone prepared to leave there and then. Twelve of the twenty staff left there and then, their spirits visibly lifted like slaves unshackled and tasting sweet freedom for the first time.

Oddly, Robin, the 12-year-old acting supervisor was among the first to go, I wish him well in his new life.

Unfortunately Robin's immediate superior did not see my actions as liberatory, but as he put it 'illegal and stupid and get out of my restaurant'.

I felt it prudent to leave then.

Today was a good day, I feel my work here is done and tonight will be my last night in Shrewsbury.

WEEK 2 DAY 4

My mother rang me. After she stopped shouting I ascertained that Toby arrived at my old home this morning.

I told her I had given him permission to live in my room, and she started shouting again, something about owning the house, axe-murderers and no longer having a son. I could tell she was upset so I hung up.

I'm sure Mother will come to see past Toby's grubby, menacing exterior and appreciate his finer qualities.

People need reminding that when life gives you lemons, you should concentrate on their cheery colour and rich vitamin C content rather than the bitter taste and acidic, stinging juices.

Spent most of today travelling, not many people spoke to me. I'm in no rush to get anywhere, which is just as well since I'm relying on public transport.

I didn't sleep very well again last night; I feel the pressure of solving the many global problems weighing heavily on my shoulders.

One of the biggest obstacles to general harmony, as I see it, is that people are too preoccupied with their own problems to worry about other people's problems.

Well I don't have any problems of my own, so I'm going to try and tackle as many belonging to other people that I can, alleviate the pressure on the general populous and thus aid international harmony.

I met a man called Stephen Hampson on the bus today; he's an office worker, much like I used to be in my former life. He told me that instead of spending his time pushing a pen, what he really wanted to do was be a professional footballer.

As gently as I could I explained to him that the likelihood of a Premier division team signing an 18 stone, 57 year-old man with inch thick spectacle lenses were quite slim and he should set his sights a bit lower.

To cut a long story short, he left me with definite plans to become a referee.

I'm sat on a bus and I just saw the most astonishing thing. A car overtook my bus, it was blue, I'm not sure of the model.

As it passed I saw the driver and I am absolutely sure it was the popular rapper Eminem.

What he is doing driving into Shropshire I don't know, perhaps researching material for a hard-hitting new rap-rock fusion concept album about Shropshire.

The bus just passed the blue car, it isn't Eminem after all, not unless he's had radical surgery recently.

WEEK 2 DAY 5

Just had a nasty emotional jar.

I never thought a road sign could trigger such melancholy, such anguish, I've just passed a sign confirmed my worst fears; I've just left Shropshire.

I've been stopping at a few smaller towns and villages, prolonging my journey and I think, subconsciously trying to stay in Shropshire for as long as possible.

Now I have forever left behind the glistening spires of Hodnet, the rugged greens of Marchamley Wood, the commercial frenzy of Market Drayton and the whimsical good folk of Bletchley.

The A529 is now no longer a mystery to me, a golden highway leading to unfathomable adventure, it is now just one of many roads I have travelled, roads that I am leaving behind.

I feel a transformation today, a new spiritual level has been reached, I am sad to leave beloved Shropshire behind, but I can continue stronger, a man with a mission, my heart swelled with inspirational ideas to better humankind and save the world from tyranny and misery, and uneven pavements.

WEEK 2 DAY 6

I accidentally got on the wrong bus today; I was aiming to find somewhere to stay in Birmingham, but ended up heading towards Wales.

Due to this, I was forced to revisit the emotional roller coaster of re-entering Shropshire.

The landscape seemed to change before me, as if the land itself were smiling to welcome me home, humming with welcoming warmth and safety.

I was just considering popping home to see how Mother and Toby were getting on when the bus left Shropshire and I was once again forced to leave Shropshire and confront my feelings once again.

Emotionally drained, I am heading back to Birmingham, but taking a circuitous route to avoid the sensual allure of my homeland.

I have to put personal feelings aside if I am really going to make any difference.

WEEK 2 DAY 7

Staying in a 2 star hotel in Birmingham, at least I think it's a 2 star.

The sign outside has two gold stars and a third stain where it looks like a star has fallen off.

I didn't like to ask the manager if this was because it had just dropped off or been deliberately stripped from the hotel by tourism officials.

Judging from the communal bathroom, I suspect the latter.

Toby rang me today, he was very grateful for my help and has settled in at my old home. It gave me a real feeling of well-being to hear someone tell me I had changed their life.

The first of many. Once my Mother's initial hysteria died down,

she apparently was quite welcoming and Toby has become my adoptive brother.

He is staying in my old room, and he has even applied to work at my old office, doing my old job. I warned him about the pitfalls of working in office procurement.

He told me he has met a local girl already and formed a fledgling relationship, I couldn't be happier for him and wished him well.

I felt no twinge of regret at the hole I left in Moreton Say getting filled by someone else so speedily, life is change and I have chosen to take the bull of fate by the horns of decision and ride him into Birmingham.

WEEK 3 DAY 1

Walked through Birmingham in the snow early this morning, an icing sugar dusting of virgin snow had settled over wealthy and poor alike.

I had no idea Birmingham was so beautiful. When I have heard people talk of Birmingham they say dirty, industrial, concrete, tense, but when I saw the streets of

Birmingham this morning it was icy fresh, tasty, new and full of goodness, like a giant brummie sorbet.

Saw a man asleep in a skip, next to him a luxury car. I'm not sure what make the car was, but it looked expensive, the skip was a large open skip, one of the 12 cubic yard capacity red and yellow ones like a builders skip but with higher sides. The icy dusting made the sleeping man and the expensive car look equally exquisite. I woke the sleeping man, who looked like Stan Kirsch, only older and asked him if I could buy him breakfast, hoping perhaps to find what ills troubled Birmingham and how I might tackle them. His strange dialect was initially difficult to understand so I followed him down a nearby alley, this turned out to be a mistake.

It was an hour later when I woke up, blood crusted on my forehead and a stabbing pain in my side, where, as it turned out, I'd been stabbed. My wallet had been taken from my pocket, I had prepared for this eventuality and concealed most of my cash in my left shoe. Unfortunately my shoes were also gone.

I was taken to Accident and Emergency, nothing serious wrong with me but they say something stabbed me in the side and knocked me on the head. The authorities refute my suggestions that I may have slipped on the ice hitting my head and landing on a knife-like object, and then perhaps some opportunistic children may have taken my shoes for a joke, they seem to think the man in the skip mugged me. I admit that's a possibility, but like to keep an open mind about things and will not be pressing charges.

I discharged myself and got a taxi back to the hotel. I need to sleep now.

WEEK 3 DAY 2

The snow outside has melted into a grey slush, Birmingham is horrible.

Didn't leave the hotel room today, I removed the dressings myself and it looks a lot worse then I imagine it really is. My body is bruised and punctured but my spirit is full of fire and determination. I found if I moved the hotel television onto the bed, I could watch TV in the mirrors reflection from the bath, so I caught up on world events, Trisha and Neighbours.

Room Service is incredibly expensive, so I made a modest meal out of complimentary tea, coffee, instant hot chocolate, oat biscuits and UHT milk. Supplies were low by eleven, but I was able to liberate some extra biscuits from the maid's trolley.

Tried to get hold of Tony Blair again on the telephone, couldn't even get to talk to Gregory this time. I'm beginning to suspect that my message of peace has not been passed on, this would explain George Bush's aggressive stance, and he scares even me. I think I might travel to America next and see what effect I can have there, bring a little of that Moreton Say magic to my colonial cousins.

WEEK 3 DAY 3

My mother rang me this morning. I was weak from two days of biscuits, tiny cartons of milk and instant chocolate. I told her I was in Madrid looking into some human-rights violations and couldn't talk right now.

I rang a travel agent and booked the cheapest ticket to the States that they had, a cancellation flight to Alabama. It leaves Heathrow in four days, weather permitting, so I'm going to go out now and buy some travel clothes and new shoes. I'm leaving the room right now. Goodbye.

I'm back. I made it as far as the Hotel bar, bought six bags of crisps and some dry-roasted peanuts before running back to my room. I need to shake out of this mood. The room has become a safe womb for me, a secure haven in what I perceive as an unsafe city, and I need to snap out of this right now. My masterplan was to travel, discover, enlighten and free, how can I free others from their fears and repression if I can't get past the lobby?

Found myself thinking longingly of office consumable order forms today, life was so much simpler just a few weeks ago when it revolved around photocopiers, paperclips and four-hole punches. Never again will I marvel at the sleek grey design of an E440 heavy duty stapler. Still, no great achievement was ever made without some measure of sacrifice.

WEEK 3 DAY 4

In hunger and desperation I rang room service and tried to order food. The woman who answered the phone might as well have been speaking Japanese for all the sense she made, after five minutes of increasingly frenzied attempts to have a desert of some description brought to my room I gave in.

I've not really travelled that far by world standards, Telford is only about 30 miles west, but already the changes in dialect make communication difficult, the only thing Room Service did seem to offer me that I understood was "arse cream" which I didn't require. It occurred to me just now she may have meant 'ice cream'. Damn, I like ice cream.

One positive thing I did do today, I cut my toenails. They had got quite long and since I had some time on my hands, I was able to fashion a quite exquisite rose from the curled toenail clippings. I think I'll leave it as a gift for the maid.

WEEK 3 DAY 5

Saw a demonstration on the news where 750 women in Australia stripped naked and formed a heart and an anti-war slogan from their bodies. I found this incredibly inspirational and finally left my hotel room. Motivated by their brave nude sentiments, I walked into the busiest shopping precinct I could find and took off my anorak and then my jumper while shouting "Say No To War!" as loudly as I could manage. No-one really paid much attention and it was very cold so I put my clothes back on.

So I went to a department store café instead. I chose the cafe so they would not mistake my lone anti-war protest for not being able to find a changing room. I just started to get my top off and security asked and then propelled me to leave before I really managed to get my point across about saying no to war.

In the evening I found my way back to the skip where I'd tried to buy the man who looked like an older Stan Kirsch some breakfast. He was still there, fast asleep and wearing my shoes. To show I bore him no ill will, I did buy him a breakfast bap from a café and left it next to him in the skip with a brief note explaining my quest for global harmony and the basic premise of goodness that drives me.

"Hello friend.

My name is Morris Telford; you may remember me from a few days ago, I woke you up offered to buy you breakfast and then had an accident in the nearby alley. I am currently travelling the world trying to improve it.

It has been suggested to me that you mugged me, violated my rights, stole my possessions and left me for dead. I believe in the basic good nature of all people so I'm sure this is not the case and it was simply a misunderstanding. I've left you some breakfast (under this note) and I hope this simple gesture restores your faith in human nature. I can see from your current sleeping arrangements that times are difficult and hope things improve for you, that fine pair of shoes you now wear propel you to self-betterment and next time our paths cross you are happy, healthy and less violent. Try to rise like a refuse covered phoenix from the fires of misfortune, using my example as a lighter fluid.

All the best, Morris.

P.S. you ever visit Moreton Say, I've left my Mother's address, pop in for some tea."

I felt it was prudent not to wake him. Forgiveness is so much easier than confrontation, and I need to be up early tomorrow to catch my train.

WEEK 3 DAY 6

I'm on the train to London; there's just me and a family of five in this carriage. There must be fifty seats in here but the three delightful children have decided to sit next to me.

They are called Brad, George and Keanu, the mother and father look so proud, it's hard to imagine why. I did try to explain to them about what I'm doing but they seem more interested in my opinion on Wrestling Federations, though strangely they have never heard of Big Daddy or Giant Haystacks.

I'm hiding the palmtop now, the three boys seem to think it's a Gameboy and keep trying to grab it.

I pretended to be asleep for most of the journey, this was oddly stressful and tiring, the boys kept poking me.

Met a man at Heathrow that works in a small airport shop that sells nothing but Ties. He was called James and looked like a younger Hilary Clinton. I told him I find it hard to believe that he can make a living just selling ties and he said he found it hard to believe I was in my thirties and never left Shropshire before.

This afforded me an excellent opportunity to explain to him the cocoon of joy that is Moreton Say and how I want to make the whole world one big Moreton Say where everyone is nice to each other.

He didn't seem very interested until I started buying ties from him, then after three hours chatting and 97 tie purchases he solemnly promised to promote kindness and love for the rest of his days. Another triumph.

WEEK 3 DAY 7

My plane flies in three hours, I'm sat in the airport lounge waiting. There's a funny smell here, hard to explain, it's chemical yet human, a mixture of impatient sweat and disinfectant. And orange cordial.

I've just found out that Alabama has a Birmingham too, a sign of some sort surely?

Just before getting on the plane Toby rang, he starts work at my old office tomorrow, doing the job I forsook to save mankind. He also told me he is 'seeing' the woman who lives next door, my lovely Sophia. I had to turn the phone off before he could tell me much more, but obviously I am very happy for him. And for Sophia.

I'm on the plane now; I've never flown before. My mother suggested I suck butterscotch when we take off, I can't remember why. I didn't have any butterscotch so I sucked on the complimentary headphones instead. I've given a tie to each of my fellow travellers as an ice-breaker (a tie-breaker?) and they seem a fine collection of people, though most of them are too tired to talk to me for long.

This time tomorrow, I'll be in Alabama, Toby will be ordering paperclips and the world will still need my help. I must not rest until all of America know of me, the good will know my message of peace and the evil will know my retribution. I hope Toby remembers to allow for seasonal fluctuations in ordering stationary, I'll ring him when we land.

WEEK 4 DAY 1

Real American drizzle greeted me as the plane landed at Birmingham International Airport, Alabama. No-one was there to meet me, thankfully the world press has yet to get wind of my quest for world harmony so I am not yet hounded by paparazzi or hindered by the unwanted attentions of big business wanting a slice of Moreton Say.

As soon as we landed I rang Toby.

He was out.

With Sophia.

The men at customs seemed very nice at first, smartly dressed, short hair, uniforms. They reminded me of the West Mercia police in Shropshire, a wise and noble organisation and a protective force to be reckoned with.

I know the world is full of violence and lawlessness, but I'd like to see Saddam Hussain or Al Capone or Snoop Doggy Dog try to park their car illegally in Market Drayton, they wouldn't know what had hit them.

I'd never seen a real firearm before and asked a customs officer if I could have a look at his. This seemed to agitate them and I regret reaching for the gun before receiving permission from him. After they let me get up off the ground they took me to one side and began searching my bag.

They seemed particularly interested in my notebook and asked a lot of questions about the doodle I had done on page seven. It was supposed to be a bingo marker, but I can see why they might have thought it looked like a missile. Apparently just after I left there was some security alert at Heathrow. The trouble really started when I told them about how I met a man from Tie-Rack at Heathrow airport, I think they misheard what I said.

There has been some talk of deporting me, but I do get to spend the night in custody so at least it's free accommodation.

WEEK 4 DAY 2

I spent my first ever night in the cells last night. It wasn't so bad. I felt a bit like Ronnie Barker in 'Porridge', only instead of Richard Beckinsale there was a man in the cell next door who thought he was Celine Dion.

I'm 97% sure he wasn't, although his rendition of 'My Heart Will Go On' did make me weep sweet tears of joy.

The officers here have been very nice to me. Robert, who looks like a younger Trevor McDonald, rang my Mother who verified who I am.

They tell me they just need to 'further check the authenticity of my story'; and then I can go. They certainly seem calmer having spoken to my mother; she does have a very calming, though slightly nasal, voice.

I've been alone most of the day, still waiting to hear when I can go. I've promised to go and see Celine in Las Vegas if they release him in time to fulfil his contractual obligations there.

WEEK 4 DAY 3

They let me go. I've got my bag back, my passport back, but best of all my freedom back.

The open sky above me is clear blue and I never, ever want to be incarcerated again.

The sky in Alabama looks exactly like the sky in Moreton Say. Everything else is different.

Alabama is so different from Shropshire it's almost like another country. They have buildings that defy all reason, taller even than the high-rise flats in the other Birmingham, but all the lifts work and there is no smell of urine.

The people, while more coherent than some I met in the other Birmingham, talk with an odd drawl, as if someone else was dragging the words from their throats. This is what people call the 'Deep South' of America, so it must be like the Cornwall of the USA, I've never been to Cornwall but I suspect there are many similarities.

The food here is always so big. You ask for a sandwich and you get a loaf, you ask for a burger and you get the better portion of a whole cow. I asked for some teacake in a café and they had no idea what it was, hard to believe such a developed country can't provide it's people with toasted teacake.

The waitress, told me Bingo is illegal in some parts of America, but gave me directions to the Players Delight Bingo Hall, I'm very excited.

WEEK 4 DAY 4

I'm staying in a hotel again, it's very nice but almost completely devoid of any personality.

I used to work with a man called Royston who collected models of trams and played the Tuba, the hotel reminds me of him. It's very nice, but with a dark, empty, bottomless pit at it's heart.

I go to play Bingo today. The noble sport of Bingo is an excellent way to meet people, and in Moreton Say is the primary form of social interaction. It both brings people of a common mind together in convivial surroundings and helps to discipline the mind.

I'm surprised that Bingo is illegal in some parts of America; they seem to classify it as gambling, which is of course wrong.

I've been playing Bingo since I was seven, sometimes the vicar called the numbers, so how can it possibly be gambling? It's a game of skill and determination, of fury and passion, and never underestimate the advantage of a superior quality bingo marker.

The inscrutable art of Bingo is the king of pastimes, the Elvis Presley of Church Hall gatherings and I am leaving the hotel now for the Players Delight Bingo Hall and my first taste of the sacred cards for over a month.

I'm taking "Elvira" one of my favourite bingo markers, she glides across those boxes like a thing possessed.

WEEK 4 DAY 5

I've only just got back. The Players Delight Bingo Hall was quite an eye-opener.

The people have taken the pure beauty of Bingo and warped it beyond all recognition. There was a foul stench of greed in the air and a stale atmosphere of lost dreams and bitter lives.

No-one really talked very much, I always thought the mental agility needed to mark your card and chat at the same time was one of the main joys, not so in Alabama.

One old lady was playing eight cards at once and when I sat next to her and tried to introduce myself she wailed like a banshee and two men in Tuxedos made me move.

At one point I left my table to go to the toilet, when I returned "Elvira" was gone.

The theft of another man's marker is an unspeakable crime in Shropshire Bingo circles, akin to stealing a man's horse in the Old West, but within half an hour of entering the Players Delight Bingo Hall I was markerless.

None of this would ever happen in Shropshire.

The Bingo went on until quite late, I didn't win anything but I did get 19 new complimentary bingo markers for my collection, all American ones with bevelled nibs and fluorescent ink, so the evening was not a complete loss.

I wrote an Email to the local newspaper today to alert them to my presence, perhaps they will give me a lead on some problems I can tackle.

WEEK 4 DAY 6

Unable to make it to any of the Anti-War marches today I decided to make a personal statement.

I had 1000 A4 posters printed. Yellow paper and bold black text.

'Be nice to each other like people are in Shropshire'
- (Morris Telford)

My original slogan was a lot longer but they charge per word.

I rode to the top of one of the tallest skyscrapers I could find today. The view from the roof was outstanding, a sweeping vista of manmade towers. A man was standing near the edge looking down to the streets below, I naturally assumed he was about to jump and ran over to stop him. As I wrapped my arms around his legs and started screaming, "Don't do it", I realised he had a harness on.

The only jumping going on was my own, to conclusions.

His name was Bucky and he cleans windows, he was a window cleaner. Bucky looked like a younger Chewbacca, all hair and growls, but after we cleared up the misunderstanding he offered me a ride.

He has a great job, the wind in his hair, no-one looking over his shoulder, as much windolene as he can carry home.

Oddly, Bucky hated his job so I convinced him to change occupation; he is now pursuing a career in Dental Hygiene. Before he handed in his notice we were able to plaster all 1000 of my posters on the outside of the building, which was great because it made them nearly impossible to remove from the inside.

Now all those office workers will be greeted with the intriguing message "Be nice to each other like people are in Shropshire" and hopefully some of them will have the good sense to take my words to heart, perhaps visit Shropshire and taste the joy for themselves.

WEEK 4 DAY 7

No reply from the newspaper yet so I decided to take more positive action. I made a large sign that said, "Ask me if I can help, I will be your friend" and walked to what seemed like an impoverished neighbourhood. People practically ran away from me.

Went back to the hotel. The hotel television has an astounding number of channels with almost no actual content to any of them.

I've been reading the kind words from people nice enough to leave me a message on the BBC Shropshire website.

I'm slightly disturbed by Tim's enthusiasm, I do not want to become a messiah figure for office consumable clerks the world over, if you were all to follow my example right now, who would order all the paperclips? Instead try and find your own path, though I am happy to offer advice.

I am stunned that the author Paul McAvoy would imply that my weblog is fabricated. I have given up everything to follow a dream and my road ahead needs to be paved with the flagstones of hope and freedom, not the uneven gravel of doubt and fantasy. The truth is stranger than fiction, unless of course you read a lot of science fiction and fantasy novels.

I'm very glad James the Shropshire Lad has brought to my attention the problem of IGMT building all over Ironbridge. I have Emailed IGMT and demanded an explanation.

If it requires my personal attention I will put it on my list. Thanks to Mike Batt for the advice on hitchhiking, it does seem an excellent way of meeting people and I shall adopt it as my main means of travel.

I won't however be buying a money belt as they make me look stupid, I find it much more sensible to keep cash in my shoe. Thanks for the advice Mike, and for all the wonderful Wombles records you gave us over the years.

WEEK 5 DAY 1

I've been watching television for 7 hours straight now.

Each time one channel loses its interest, there are 137 others waiting for my attention. I saw a program about a man who was so overweight he had to have his front upstairs window removed and be hoisted from his bedroom by a crane.

I thought the look on his face as he saw open sky above him for the first time in 11 years was the most moving thing I had ever seen.

That is until I stumbled upon channel 98 – the 24 hour prize bingo channel, they had markers on there the likes of which Tony "two fat ladies" Codling himself has never seen. It's hard to believe I managed for all those years in Moreton Say with just five channels, six if you count S4C.

It occurred to me that if they can manage to fill 137 channels every day, they produce enough TV in three days to fill a whole year. This got me thinking. We must have produced more films and television shows than one person could ever possibly watch in a lifetime, so why make any more?

Just have a seventy or eighty year cycle of repeats and then all the people that spend time making all the films and TV shows could spend their time feeding the hungry, building better housing, improving sanitation and doing good deeds.

I'm going to write to all the major film companies and networks and see what they think.

Last night in the Hotel today, tomorrow I start hitchhiking.

WEEK 5 DAY 2

On reflection, I hadn't really thought the whole seventy year media cycle through properly.

If you repeated the news people would notice, you'd have to keep making news programmes - and Countdown.

Up to the day I left Moreton Say I had seen every episode of Countdown ever made, from the day Channel 4 started, a fine programme and the only remaining safe haven on British television for Richard Stilgoe.

I begin my hitchhiking odyssey across the USA this morning, according to the hotel desk clerk, Rodney, who looks quite astonishingly like a 1960s Robert Wagner, the truckers are my best chance of a long ride so I'm going to a roadside diner frequented by truck drivers.

I've seen the film Convoy so I expect to fit in quite well.

WEEK 5 DAY 3

The casual camaraderie of the trucking fraternity so evident in the film Convoy does not seem to exist in Alabama.

I ordered a pot of tea at the diner and offered to buy breakfast for anyone willing to give me a lift somewhere.

My biggest mistake was trying to emulate the CB Radio talk I assumed all truckers use and my overuse of terms like 'good buddy', '10-4' and 'rubber duck' seemed to give the wrong impression and I found myself in an enclosed space with 50 large tattooed men who thought I was making fun of them.

Buying everyone breakfast seemed to calm them down and a man called Shirley with a shaven head and arms as thick as my neck welcomed me into his cab. He isn't much of a talker.

I just called home today for the first time in a few days. No-one was in.

Shirley is smoking a long green cigar that smells of turpentine. The truck cab is filled with an acrid smoke and I'm not allowed to wind a window down.

I think my eyes are bleeding. I tried to tell Shirley about my mission to help people, make the world a better place to be in, but his life philosophy seems to be repeating the phrase - 'don't talk to me pinhead' which makes connecting on a spiritual level quite difficult.

Shirley dropped me off at a motel, which is like a hotel but spelt incorrectly.

Before he dropped me off I did learn one thing about Shirley; he's a woman.

I told her she had beautiful eyes as I left the truck and for a moment beneath the bald, muscular exterior I saw a frightened little girl.

Called home again. No answer. I hope everyone is alright, Mother seldom goes out during the day for longer than 45 minutes, the time it takes to walk to the chemists and back allowing time to buy some Tunes, a tooth-friendly lollipop and renew her prescription.

Once, in 1996, she was gone for nearly an hour, but that was only because a tractor hit her.

WEEK 5 DAY 4

Called home again. Everyone is fine. Toby was good enough to take Mother and Aunt Felicity for a meal in Market Drayton as a thankyou for their kindness and hospitality. Such a nice gesture, I can see my instincts about Toby were accurate.

I could never get Mother or Aunt Felicity to venture as far afield as Market Drayton, so I'm obviously very happy that Toby could achieve this.

I'm going to walk down the roadside and see what travel companions fate brings to me.

WEEK 5 DAY 5

For reasons of National Security I can't write down what happened today.

WEEK 5 DAY 6

For reasons of National Security I can't write down what happened today.

WEEK 5 DAY 7

For reasons of National Security I can't write down what happened today.

Woke up this morning on the side of the highway. My bottom was sore and my head hurt. I had the sort of headache I have only experienced once before, when I was mistakenly given sherry trifle at my seventeenth birthday party and jumped off the shed shouting "I can fly mother. I can fly like an eagle" before passing out. Someone, (I'm pretty sure it wasn't me, I don't really know what National Security is), has completed my diary entries for the past three days with the words-

"For reasons of National Security I can't write down what happened today."

The last thing I remember was thumbing a lift from a limousine with little flags stuck on the front, I can only presume that the American government have subjected me to some sort of memory loss drug to erase all recollection of the brain washing I have been subjected to. Someone has stolen three days of my life and I want him or her back.

I am not going to take this sort of violation lying down and have written a stern Email to George Bush.

"Dear Mr Bush,

I've tried to contact you several times on the telephone and am disappointed you were unable to take my calls personally.

My name, as I am sure you are aware by now, is Morris Telford.

I am writing to complain about the recent mistreatment I have received at the hands of one of your covert organisations, the CIA, FBI, MIB I'm not sure which but they had a car with little flags on. I was abducted for three days and have no memory, just a sore head and posterior.

Please don't pretend you don't know what I'm talking about, I know all about 'plausible deniability'. Where I come from (Moreton Say, Shropshire, England, UK) we don't have 'plausible deniability, we have truth, honesty, justice and unless you count my seventeenth birthday party we don't give people perception altering substances or meddle with their bottoms against their will.

You might think that you can do what you want just because you are President, well you can't. I once knew an office assistant who thought he could change the whole way that photocopier toner was ordered just because he had the authority to do so. Well he did change the process, but it was wrong and nearly jeopardised a very important presentation when copies of a handout with a picture of a pig in a suit started to come out grey. Please don't let history repeat itself.

If I have anymore unexplained blackouts I will hold you personally responsible.

Yours truly,

M.Telford"

I've taken some orange flavour junior aspirin. I feel confident that the stern tone of my correspondence should do the trick and resume my hitchhiking today with renewed determination.

WEEK 6 DAY 2

A young man called Brad driving his pick-up truck picked me up this morning. I tried to explain to him the inherent humour in him 'picking me up' in a 'pick-up' but he made me get out after less than a mile when I refused to stop trying to explain to him how funny it was.

American humour seems to differ from the sense of humour in Shropshire.

My feet are hurting; I've been walking for miles now. The soles of my shoes are started to get sticky as they melt and my toes burn with every step. The cash I keep in my shoe is not going to be legal tender much longer if I keep it there.

I managed to walk to a petrol station. They call them Gas stations in Alabama, which is odd, because petrol is clearly a liquid and not a gas. I tried to explain to the attendant but his expression started to look like Brad's had earlier so I didn't press the point. I explained to the attendant, who looked like a young, blonde Harry Dean Stanton and was called Jerry, who I was and asked if he needed any help. Jerry told me he needed $1000 to buy some "stuff", so I gave it him.

Then I saw something very ugly in Jerry's eyes, a flame of greed I have never seen in Harry Dean Stanton's eyes, even when he was doing a bewilderingly out-of-place cameo. Jerry took my $1000 and said something about what would really help sort his problems would be $10,000 for "more stuff", I could smell his regret at not asking for more first time around. I asked him if he could be more specific about what kind of "stuff" he had in mind and his imagination failed him, so I left before he got angry with me.

Funny how giving someone money can just make them unhappy.

I'm sleeping under the stars tonight; it's getting quite cold now. An animal of some sort ran past earlier, then a naked Hannah Gordon ran past after the animal trying to spear it with a paintbrush, she turned to me and said "Morris, you've won the box of watercolours". I think I might have a touch of heatstroke.

It's three in the morning now and I'm regretting not buying a tent, or a sleeping bag, or one of those shiny blankets, or some walking boots, instead my camping equipment so far consists of an airline inflatable pillow and three Twinkies. I couldn't sleep so I'm walking to keep warm, and I seem to be hitchhiking down a road nobody ever uses. I can't understand why such a big road is so quiet.

Jerry passed me on his way home; he offered me a lift for $250. I declined his offer.

WEEK 6 DAY 3

Jerry came back and gave me a lift to the next town and took me to a hotel he recommended. He apologised for the way he had acted and I gave him some valuable information about how people treat each other in Shropshire, how money will never buy you happiness and how the only currency of any real value was love.

I thought he had taken it to heart but he asked for $20,000 for a life-saving operation to his spleen just before he left and I think this showed his motivations were dishonest. I told him to use the NHS like everyone else.

I've decided not to just give out money, people need more direct help and I am not being responsible just handing out cash.

In saying that, I did meet an old woman today called Maureen. Maureen's goal in life seemed to be collecting empty cans in a shopping trolley and pushing the trolley around. I asked her why she did this and she said that the more aluminium she keeps near her, the less likely it was the government would find her.

She actually put forward a very convincing argument so I bought her a used Audi with an all-aluminium body shell and she lives there now.

Maureen seemed very interested in Moreton Say and I gave her my Mother's address in case she ever visits Shropshire, which seems unlikely as apparently the government took away her passport in 1978 for 'knowing too many secrets'. Maureen was one of the nicest people I have met so far in Alabama, and yet she lives on the fringe of society. Funny how the souls that have been most rejected by us often have the most to offer.

Than again, Maureen had a friend called Brent who just foamed at the mouth and threw his shoes at me, so sometimes these souls are rejected with good reason.

WEEK 6 DAY 4

Stayed in the hotel, had a nice meal in the restaurant. I hate eating alone so I asked a young couple if I could join them. Amazingly they were from Shropshire, Harris and Joanne Kettle from Oswestry. I should have known they were from Shropshire; they were the fifteenth table in the restaurant that I asked to join and the first to say yes. Their accent was a bit odd though.

They were very welcoming and talking to them about the magical, faraway land of Shropshire reminded me of why I was alone in a hotel in Alabama.

I'm not here to wallow in self-pity or dwell on failure, I'm here to inject some Shropshire positivity into the strange folk of the world not fortunate enough to have been born in Shropshire, like a hypodermic full of joy piercing the veins of humanity.

Harris and Joanne gave up their precious holiday time together to talk to a complete stranger, I cannot thank them enough.

Fortunately I was able to help them, Joanne needed to fly home again urgently to see her sick Uncle so I gave her the $1000 for her flight and the $3500 she needed for travelling expenses, the least I could do for such a nice lady.

They also invited me up to their room for a nightcap, but I was concerned I had overstayed my welcome and left them to their Alabama Pecan Pie desserts.

WEEK 6 DAY 5

I saw Harris and Joanne talking, shaking hands and laughing with Jerry in the hotel carpark this morning; I hope Jerry doesn't take advantage of their good nature.

I went shopping and bought some camping equipment. I found a collapsible tent that folds down to the size of my fist, some walking boots that people use for mountain climbing and one of those shiny blankets that keep you warm if you are cold and cold if you are warm, like a thermos you can climb inside.

No one ever seems to reply to my Emails in America. None of the TV networks, newspapers or politicians has got back to me yet so I really appreciate all the Email support from home.

Mike Batt has written again, Hi Mike. You are quite right about the cream teas and pasties, it's impossible to get either in Alabama. In one Alabama café I ordered a cream tea and a pastie, I was given a cup of tea with cream instead of milk and a Danish pastry, hardly the same. The waitress was six feet tall with one eyebrow and a pierced chin so I didn't complain. Sorry I confused you with the legendary Wombling Mike Batt, thank you for putting me straight. Why should I avoid truckers with red lights in their cabs?

I was very moved by the 'Ode to Mr T' from M(via Tibberton). I have yet to receive a reply from IGMT regarding their building plans for Ironbridge. It's on my list of things to do so rest assured the problem will be addressed.

Thanks to Joe Summerfield for your kind offer of Shropshire cuisine at your Uncle Bing and Auntie Sheila's in Frederick, MA. I shall put that on my list also.

WEEK 6 DAY 6

Spent most of today with a trucker called Ahab. He bore an uncanny resemblance to Brian May, only with a long, wispy beard that would surely have become entangled in the strings of any guitar he played. Ahab played country music loud enough to make my ears bleed and sang along with wild enthusiasm.

I'm not a very big fan of country music, obviously I acknowledge the talents of Billy Ray "achy breaky heart" Cyrus but the rest leaves me cold. I once went to a line dancing class in Market Drayton village hall and an eleven-year-old girl broke my ankle during the "Bear Mountain Hop".

Ahab is married with eleven children; I offered to drive his truck for him while he visited his family. He told me he hadn't been home for six years and that was the secret of a good relationship. It was hard to argue with his logic, but I tried anyway, it didn't work. He showed me a photograph of his family, oddly his wife looked like Freddie Mercury, moustache and all.

I called home and spoke to Toby. He's doing very well now, he told me he has been promoted already, I'm obviously very happy for him. I worked there for over a decade and was never promoted and Toby gets promoted after a few weeks. So it's really, really good to see Mr Magson has turned over a new leaf and started recognising potential in his staff, maybe it was my leaving that made him reconsider his management style. Toby also started to tell me how well he is getting on with

Sophia, I really wanted to hear more but phone calls home are so expensive I told him I had to go.

I'm sleeping in my new tent by the roadside now, the stars are so clear out here with no light pollution it's like thousands of little aliens are shining their flashlights at me. I can almost hear them whisper in their alien voices, sounding a bit like Stephen Hawking "What are you doing down there Morris?" and I poke my head out of the tent and shout in reply "I'm all alone in a world of madmen trying to show them how easy it is to be happy. I'm a dazzling beacon of purity in a world tainted by country music and greed. Come and visit Moreton Say before you think about invading earth, you'll never want to leave."

I wish I had someone to play Bingo with.

WEEK 6 DAY 7

Sunny day today so I hope to meet some interesting people in need of a little of my special Shropshire magic.

An elderly man called Jim stopped his camper van to pick me up. Jim is a fascinating man; he resembles an older Simon Callow, only without the nose and continually smoking a cigar. Jim used to be a soldier and had some horrific stories to tell about his active service. He once had to eat his own foot, not as you might imagine out of hunger, but out of sheer boredom. He also told me he knew seventy-three different ways to kill a man, I asked him if he had a favourite and he told me it had to be number twenty-eight – "The spoon". He didn't elaborate.

Just before he dropped me off Jim showed me his collection of antique firearms. He said antique, but the laser sights, automatic machine loaders and computerised targeting on some of his weapons led me to believe some were relatively recent. The camper van was packed with all sorts of weapons with a little foldaway bed in the middle of it all and an old poster of The 'A' Team on the wall. Jim insisted that his collection was just an innocent hobby and he only ever used his fiery arsenal of death for "personal protection", I didn't feel inclined to argue as he was holding a missile launcher at the time.

Aside from his lethal hobby, Jim actually seemed like a nice man, a devout vegetarian and committed ecologist, admittedly a devout vegetarian and committed ecologist with enough firepower to level Market Drayton and a fixation with George Peppard, but a nice man. Jim kindly offered to address any issues I had with IGMT and Ironbridge but I suspect his idea of direct action might prove structurally damaging to Ironbridge itself so I declined.

As Jim drove off into the Alabama sunset, I thought it's good to have a man like Jim on my side.

WEEK 7 DAY 1

I explained to a busker today what I do with my life now.

He told me my motives were good, but that just one man can't possibly make a difference.

I told him to tell that to Isambard Kingdom Brunel, to Albert Einstein, to Isaac Newton, to Abraham Lincoln, to Lord Clive of India, to Thomas Telford. I had to explain to him who a couple of them were.

He told me he couldn't tell it to them as they were all dead and would I please go and make a difference somewhere else. On reflection I probably caught him at a bad time, I interrupted "Eleanor Rigby" to talk to him. As I walked away he started playing it again, but changed the word 'lonely' to 'crazy', I think he may have been referring to me.

Can one man make a difference? I might not be able to change the life of every single person, but if I can just alter one life for the better then it's all been worthwhile.

I also met a woman call Freda today who looked a bit like my old Geography teacher, Mrs Perry, only a bit thinner. Freda told me the thing she most wanted in life was to find true love, she has had a string of relationships that have all ended badly and wanted to find her 'knight in shining amour'. (sic) Though I am not perhaps as well versed in the ways of love as I might be, I did my best for her, I bought her an airline ticket to England and told her to try Market Drayton on market day, there's always a few eligible farmers there.

I hope I make a difference with Freda.

WEEK 7 DAY 2

When I was a younger man, my main concerns were the next episode of Blake's Seven, catching a glimpse of Sophia through the net curtains and Oxy-cuting my entire body. I was unaware of the suffering that goes on in the world, unaware that by chance of birth I was one of the privileged few.

Most people have no phone, no TV, have never ordered a Pizza, do not have clean water or a flush toilet. Only 40,389 People live in Shropshire out of six billion worldwide, that's just one in 148,555 people, it's all so unfair. I obviously can't bring everyone to Shropshire, there just isn't room and the foot traffic would cause havoc with the country paths. So I'm bringing Shropshire to them.

I set up a little piece of Shropshire today in a place called Hueytown.

They have a lovely park here, Martin Luther King Park, so I found a bench, set up a couple of signs saying "Morris Telford's Corner Of Shropshire", I displayed my Ordinance Survey Map of Shropshire on a nearby tree, made sandwiches, brought some lemonade, played Chas n 'Dave tapes in the background (it's all I had) and waited for the floods of curious Americans.

After a couple of hours not one person had approached me, most walked on the grass to avoid me. I decided to take a more aggressive approach and began shouting at some girl's playing rounders nearby. They call it softball here, or baseball, but it's actually rounders. The girls shouted some things back but the things they shouted were both unhelpful and obscene so I left the park.

I'm going to try again tomorrow but without the music or sandwiches, I think the people were overwhelmed by my generosity and the complex lyrics of Charles and

David. This triggered suspicion and fear. I'm also going to dress more smartly, perhaps wear a tie, or some trousers.

I was wearing trousers today, just not smart ones.

WEEK 7 DAY 3

I've set up "Morris Telford's Corner Of Shropshire" in Martin Luther King Park again today. I got here early to catch the pre-work dog walkers and so far eight people have spoken to me and four people smiled as they hurried past. To be fair, on top of those twelve, seventy-eight people have totally ignored me, twenty three people have asked me to leave them alone, ten people have sneered at me in a very negative manner, two people asked me if I was ill and one person thought I was their dead husband. They were mistaken.

A little girl came up to me, one of the few not snatched away by parents suspicious of my Shropshire extravaganza. She was called Ruby; she was nearly nine and looked like she might grow up to resemble Barbara Windsor, only taller.

I told her I travel the world helping solve problems, a bit like Edward Woodward in 'The Equaliser' only younger and without the trench coat or killing people. Ruby had never heard of Mr Woodward or indeed his equalising exploits but she did tell me that her hamster, Rocky, had died last week and wanted my help. While I admit that raising the dead is currently beyond my abilities as a champion of justice, promoter of village life and scourge of evil, I felt it my duty to try and ease her youthful grief.

Showing the little girl my Ordinance Survey Map that I'd pinned to a tree, I explained that I come from a faraway land called Shropshire. A magical place where all the hamsters that have done a good job of being a pet in America come to when they die.

In Shropshire the hamsters are treated like extra special guests by all the people. They have solid silver hamster wheels on every street corner, all the shops give away hamster food in little golden bags, everyone is very, very careful where they tread, those plastic spheres that people lock hamsters inside are illegal on penalty of death, the streets are paved with sawdust and the insides of toilet rolls, and there is a restraining order that means Freddie Starr can't come within 80 miles.

I told Ruby that her little pal Rocky was probably there now sat on a little hamster cushion with his name embroidered on it, filling his little cheeks full of his favourite food and listening to whatever it is hamsters like to listen to. Something by Mike Batt perhaps, or Hamster Rap, Coolio dressed as a Gerbil wearing three inch thick gold chains singing "Livin' in a Hamster's Paradise".

Despite her tender years, Ruby saw through my fabricated vision of hamster utopia. She knew full well that Rocky was not in Shropshire, he was in a shoebox in her back garden and he was never, ever coming back. I gave her $20 to buy a new hamster and that seemed to cheer her up.

WEEK 7 DAY 4

Still in the park. I bought some plane tickets to Shropshire today and offered them up as a prize; I'd wanted to do a sort of talent show but only three people entered.

The woman who won worked in a shoe shop, her talent was she could guess someone's shoe size just by looking at them. She took three guesses to get my shoe size right, but the competition was hardly ferocious so she won.

I feel my work here is done, I can feel the wandering spirit of adventure beckoning me, and I'm going on the road again.

WEEK 7 DAY 5

Nothing much happened today.

Toby called me this morning from work, I explained to him the office policy on personal calls, especially overseas calls but he laughed it off. Things are going very well for him, he likes his job, he loves Sophia and he is very grateful to me for the helping hand I gave him. I did give him a little bit of advice about Sophia, told him to be careful not to rush things, I hope he heeds my words.

Mother and Aunt Felicity are fine; one of them bought a pottery cottage yesterday.

WEEK 7 DAY 6

I'm riding in an open top jeep with a woman called Harriet who looks a bit like Whitney Houston but talks like Michael Caine.

According to a sign we just passed, I'm not in Jefferson County anymore, I'm in Tuscaloosa. Still in Alabama I think.

The country is a bit greener here, still a pale imitation of Moreton Say, but nice nonetheless.

I saw some large birds by the road, they looked like Alsatians with wings, and Harriet said they were Buzzards. They would wreck havoc with Mothers red string peanut bird feeder.

WEEK 7 DAY 7

I haven't had much joy in getting replies from the Media in Alabama, so I'm Emailing everyone at www.tuscaloosanews.com this morning to see if anyone will respond.

My Email reads –

"Hello and Good morning everyone at Tuscaloosanews.com, My name is Morris Telford and I come from a small village in Shropshire, England called Moreton Say.

You may be wondering why I am writing to you, let me explain. I left home six weeks ago for the first time at the tender age of 33. I am travelling around the world, blown by the winds of destiny, motivated by the gentle tides of Shropshire born love and riding on the crest of my savings account that I have been accumulating since the mid-eighties for just such a quest.

I intend to single-handedly bring about world peace, change people's lives for the better, right wrongs, be a champion for the underdog and tell people all about Shropshire village life and how wonderful it is.

I've just arrived in Tuscaloosa and would like to enlighten the populous, have you any suggestions on a good area to start with? Please reply, the American media have been wholeheartedly uninterested in my personal odyssey so far. If you doubt my credentials, then read about my adventure on the BBC Shropshire Website

Thank you,

yours in anticipation,

Mr Morris Telford"

I eagerly await their reply.

Mr Batt has once again been in contact on the message board, I was worried by the request "We have too many visitors from Newcastle down here, what would be your advice to put them off?". Mike, we should all try and embrace as many different cultures and attitudes as we can, even those that see wearing a coat as a sign of weakness.

I notice Wile-E has replied to you – "What exactly is wrong with having people from Newcastle "down there"? You southern shandy drinkers should be glad to have Geordie folk there, just as Morris has set out to right the wrongs of the world, we're trying to save you lot from the evils of sheep, strange pasties, clotted cream and weak cider. We're also going to teach you all how to stop being soft sod's every time a single snowflake falls, we were all out wearing just jeans and T-shirts in the "Toon" during the last blizzards while you lot were shivering, complaining and wishing you could hibernate."

I'd hate to think I was the cause of any conflict, so why don't you both life-swap for a week, Mike can brave sub-zero temperatures in a t-shirt and Wile-E can live on clotted cream and weak cider. A little bit of understanding goes a long way. Let me know how you get on.

Mike also raises a very important issue – "The BBC are not paying you are they?". No, not so much as a complimentary Radio Shropshire pen. It's a good job I have a shoe full of cash.

WEEK 8 DAY 1

No reply from Tuscaloosa news yet, they obviously do not realise the importance of my story.

I'm in quite a large city called Tuscaloosa, which, logically enough, is in Tuscaloosa, Alabama. The people here seem very busy, no one says 'good morning' to each other in the condensed fury of the morning dash to work. No one stops to chat about the weather, or parks their tractor to exchange local gossip.

I'm following a man in a suit to see where he is in such a hurry to go, I feel today I need to stop trying to solve everyone's problems all at once and concentrate on one lucky individual for the full-on Morris Telford treatment. He's wearing a grey business suit, short dark hair, he has a brown briefcase and an embedded frown. I can barely keep up with him.

He just went into a tall office building, I'm standing next to him now in the lift, despite the fact I'm typing this on my palmtop, no one pays me the least attention. I said 'good morning' to everyone in the lift, mentioned what a fine and lovely day it was outside and the only response I got was averted eyes and a cough. The man in the grey suit is edging into the corner of the lift. For some reason lifts are called elevators in America, neither name is really accurate because as well as lifting and elevating, they drop and go down (or whatever the opposite of elevate is). It's not a very fast lift.

Floor 17, the grey suit man is getting off, so am I. I have him alone in a corridor, I just shouted 'excuse me, can I have a moment of your time?' and he speeded up. I'm going to run after him.

It's later now. I nearly caught up with the man in the grey suit, but didn't even get chance to explain that I had singled him out for a full-on Shropshire enlightenment experience. He locked himself in his office and called security.

I was forcibly extracted from the building by a very nice Security Guard called Boba who looks like Jamie Oliver might if he forsook his exotic and complicated Sainsbury's cuisine for a steady diet of steroids and weightlifting. Boba was named after a Star Wars character "Boba Fett"; his parents were big fans of the films. Sadly both his parents were killed when he was quite young; they tried to recreate lightsabers using fluorescent tubes and had a nasty and quite fatal experience. Needless to say Boba's belief in the force has waned since then.

I asked Boba what he would change about his life if he could change anything? "My name" he said, which seemed quite a simple request, I explained to him that others judge us only by the limits they set themselves and he simply had to start referring to himself as something else to effect a change. I suggested the noble name 'Morris' and he thought it was a marvellous idea, so there is now a muscle-bound Jamie Oliver look-alike patrolling the offices of Tuscaloosa bearing my name. I gave him my UK Blockbuster video card as a starting point to the many possibilities that will now open up for him as they have for me and so many other Morris's worldwide.

WEEK 8 DAY 2

I've received some very, very disturbing news.

As if George Bush, on the brink of war and not responding to my letters or Emails were not enough. As if the evils that pervade everywhere except mother Shropshire did not bear down on me sufficiently. As if the terrible suffering that people who do not live in Shropshire go through were not burden enough. As if the selfish attitude of 'me first' that I see every day on my travels were not challenge enough. I have just heard about 'Country Life' magazines article on English counties.

The inviolable reputation of Shropshire has been brought into question and all my other concerns must now be put to one side. Should 'Tuscaloosanews.com' contact me now, begging for exclusive coverage of my story, they will have to wait in turn, the uncannily accurate sights of Morris Telford's anti-injustice gun are trained at the offices of 'Country Life' magazine in London. The crosshair is squarely on the forehead of Camilla Edwards. The survey article was by Sandy Mitchell, but the foundation of these terrible slurs, the research, that was by Camilla Edwards. I suspect Camilla lives in Devon ('number one' county on their list).

The moment I heard I sent this to Arabella Youens, Country Life's 'News Editor'-

"I have heard your magazine did a survey recently that rated Shropshire as 20th out of 37 English counties.

Have you ever stood in a field near Moreton Say on a dew soaked Thursday morning and listened to the cows herald in a sunrise that would make Mike Tyson weep like a little girl? Have you ever walked the magical peaks and troughs of the land surrounding Market Drayton, your feet thanking you for every footstep on the perfect earth, your eyes thanking you for the marvel of surrounding beauty and your ears singing the praises of the gentle tranquillity mixed with a subtle yet superlative symphony of nature?

Have you ever even been to Shropshire?

Nought out of five for education, nought out of ten for arts, one out of five for wildlife diversity and only two out of ten for landscape value?

I would be cancelling my subscription to 'Country Life' immediately, if I had one.

Yours in disbelief, disgust and a genuine if grudging pity,

Morris Telford"

Nought out of five for Education? I myself was educated entirely within Shropshire and left school in 1986 with Three 'O' Levels and a CSE in Metalwork. My old Headmaster, Mr Bromley would be spinning in his grave if he heard Shropshire got nought out of ten for education, and if he were dead.

There are so many things wrong with the conclusions in this survey I can barely type for shaking my head. Nought out of ten for The Arts? Have they never seen the work of Martha Etigran? Martha lives near Oswestry and with just some paint and bobbly stick on eyes can transform a stone or large pebble into an amusing little creature. You often see her at craft fairs and can pick up an original Etigran for as little as 95p. Where else but the mighty creative empire that is Shropshire?

WEEK 8 DAY 3

I fashioned a number of placards today, all proclaiming Shropshire to be the 'number one' place to live, visit and venerate in England. I was very careful not to mention Country Life by name so as to avoid legal action.

"Don't listen to 'some' magazines, Shropshire is the finest place on earth."

"If you want to enjoy real 'Country Life', go to Shropshire, it's great!"

"Do not buy any magazines with the word "Country" in the title, just in case they say untrue things about Shropshire and infect your soul with their nasty lies."

That last placard had to be written in quite small writing because of all the words which actually made it quite effective because people came closer to read it and I was able to engage them.

WEEK 8 DAY 4

If Country life is a dark storm covering Shropshire, then I am the Weatherman. If Country Life is a disease ravaging the population of Shropshire, then I am the cure.

If Country Life is an infected boil on Shropshire's peachy bottom, then I am the lance and a course of antibiotics.

I checked as many newsstands and newsagents in Tuscaloosa as I could today. None of them seem to sell Country Life, just magazines and newspapers to do with Alabama and America, so my campaign seems to be taking effect.

WEEK 8 DAY 5

No one ever seems to reply to me. Tuscaloosa news have not replied, IGMT are silent about their building work around Ironbridge, Country Life have declined to comment on their Shropshire slurs, that man in the grey suit locked himself in an office rather than speak to me and now I am standing outside a Police station because the officers would not listen to my complaint.

I found somewhere that sold Country Life. Apparently it's a 'specialist' magazine over here, the number of Alabama residents interested in a magazine about English country life is surprisingly limited. The shop refused to remove the magazine from circulation, even after I explained about the 'best county' survey.

So I just complained to the local constabulary, (they are called 'cops' over here, like in Starsky and Hutch) and they dismissed my protests. I am obviously on a lone crusade.

I came to a solution of sorts. I bought every issue of Country Life the shop had, both of them and burned them in the street outside, a public proclamation of my disgust.

Oddly, while complaining to the police did not get their attention, setting fire to two issues of Country Life in the middle of a main highway did. I was given a caution, a fine and it was suggested I leave Tuscaloosa at my earliest convenience. I think Country Life have bought the loyalty of Tuscaloosa law enforcement with the dirty money made from spreading their lies.

WEEK 8 DAY 6

Mother rang me today, nothing much happening at home in Moreton Say. There was some excitement, apparently a foreign woman was arrested on market day Market Drayton, she was propositioning farmers. I fear that the global tendrils of immorality may even be creeping towards Shropshire now; the motherland must be kept pure.

I caught a bus and slept for most of the journey. I apologised to the man sat next to me that I had slept the journey away and not had opportunity to tell him about Moreton Say and the saturating joy of Shropshire life. He was very understanding and said he didn't mind one bit.

I'm going to stay in a hotel tonight.

WEEK 8 DAY 7

I've been sat in my room dwelling on that Country Life article again. I was reading some literature I had brought with me when it triggered a thought process.

Batman had the Joker, Superman had Lex Luthor, Penelope Pitstop had The Hooded Claw, Captain America had The Red Skull, The Fantastic Four had Galactus, Spiderman had Doctor Octopus, I have Camilla Edwards, she is the Anti-Morris. I'm sure she is a lovely person, just misguided or misinformed and I feel it is my duty to educate her on the joys of Shropshire living. She is officially on my list.

I've crossed George Bush off my list, I just saw him on the news and it's quite clear to me that he intends to start a war. I don't even think a nice holiday in Shropshire would dissuade him.

WEEK 9 DAY 1

The sun is shining with the ferocity of a five-card bingo player who needs just one more number , my pale Shropshire complexion is suffering a bit and I am forced to stay indoors. I've been looking on the Internet for signs of Camilla Edwards and how I might contact her directly. I looked on Internet Search Engines under "evil", "anti-Shropshire propaganda" and "dirty lies" and could find nothing on her.

It may not be the same person, but if you look at the credits for the 2001 children's film "Monsters Inc", under Miscellaneous it has the credit - Assistant To Co-Director: Camilla Edwards.

There's something deeply wrong somewhere.

Just to be on the safe side I feel very strongly that we should all boycott Monsters Inc, just in case. Now I come to think about it, Shropshire is not mentioned once in that film. Go and see the 1950 classic "Gone To Earth" instead. A fine film, written by a Shropshire woman, set in Shropshire and filmed in Shropshire. Who needs computer generated one-eyed monsters when you can watch the glorious Shropshire countryside coupled with the story of a beautiful but innocent country girl who loves all the creatures around her, especially her pet fox cub?

I bet Camilla Edwards wouldn't appreciate it though; she'd probably give it nought out of ten. She'd probably watch the first five minutes and go and watch a film set in Devon instead, I can't think of any decent films set in Devon, there probably aren't any.

WEEK 9 DAY 2

Much as I expected, George and Tony have ignored my advice. Instead of looking to Shropshire for an example of how to get on with each other, they have taken a course of action more in keeping with the actions of someone who knows nothing of Shropshire life. They have started bombing Iraq. I wish they hadn't, it puts a real dampener on my quest for world peace and happiness when people go starting wars.

People in Alabama seem very concerned about the war starting. They all seem to be buying supplies, water, and tinned foods and duct tape. I'm not quite sure what the duct tape is for but I bought a couple of rolls and keep them with me at all times. Just to be on the safe side.

WEEK 9 DAY 3

There was an Anti-War demonstration today so I joined in. I had kept some of my anti-Country Life banner rolled up in my bag and was able to re-use them.

On reflection, using a protest against war in Iraq as a platform to incite hatred against a magazine nobody in Alabama seems to have heard of was not my finest hour. I did get three hundred and seventy four people to sign a petition asking Country Life for a second opinion on Camilla Edwards research, but to be brutally honest, most of the people who signed it probably thought they were signing an anti-war petition.

I'll be sending the petition to Country Life anyway, at least some good can come of all this.

I got talking to a girl at the protest that was called Polka; she looked a bit like a young Mexican Judi Dench. Polka had written on her white T-Shirt in black marker pen (she'd used permanent marker in a moment of anti-war frenzy) "Don't Bomb Iran". I tried to explain to Polka that Iran wasn't getting bombed, but she misunderstood and started screaming, "it's over! It's over! ", over and over. The news that Iran was not being bombed spread like wildfire and the anti-war protest soon turned into a street party, people were celebrating the end of a short-lived bombing campaign of Iran. I climbed a lamppost and managed to convey to the crowd that Iran was not being bombed, Iraq was being bombed, someone shouted "Not there as well! Bush he is a crazy man." and the protest began again. As I left I saw Polka making the 'n' on her T-shirt into a 'q'. A small victory for truth.

I know this all sounds unlikely, but I was there, it happened, the level of confusion surrounding me is very high. I saw an elderly woman duct taping shut her front door "to protect me from the nuclear", I pointed out that not only had she just duct-taped herself out of her house, but that it was a woefully inadequate countermeasure to most weapons of mass destruction. She ignored me and climbed in her window.

WEEK 9 DAY 4

I rang home, Mother wants me to come home now a war has started. I told her that my war started the day I left, my war against any oppressor I come across, any wrongdoer I disturb, anyone called Camilla with the slightest connection to Country Life magazine, no-one is safe. Mother tried to make me promise not to try and personally sort out Saddam Hussain. I explained that though it was unlikely I'd be able to hitchhike as far as Iraq, no-one was beyond the reach of my grip of justice and it would be against my principles to make such a vow.

Apparently Toby is moving in with Sophia, she feels unsafe given the current political situation and didn't want to be alone in her house at night. I hung up before Mother explained anything about the sleeping arrangements, I'm sure Toby is just doing what any neighbour would do to make a vulnerable woman feel safe.

I once went to a café in Market Drayton where the cheese and onion pie had not been sufficiently microwaved and there was a crunchy, frozen bit in the middle, but even that did not prepare me for a restaurant I went to today that sold nothing but raw fish. They had gone to a great deal of trouble to present it on little dishes, but neglected to cook any of it.

Despite my complaints they insisted it should be raw and spurned my offer to buy them a deep fat fryer. Some people just refuse to be helped.

WEEK 9 DAY 5

I can only presume my media campaign has been overshadowed by the war in Iraq, no-one has replied to me, no-one has contacted me asking for interviews, no radio stations are fighting to get me on air, no TV stations are desperate to speak to my people and when I walk down the street, no-one notices me.

I expected to have made more of a difference by now. If anything the world is a more unsettled place now than when I set off two months ago, what am I doing wrong?

Thanks to Mike Batt for his concern about my safety, I noticed this message - "Morris where are you? Are you ok? Shall I post you a pasty?".

Mike was concerned because my BBC web diary was not updated for a few days, don't worry Mike, all is well. In answer to your question, the BBC do not currently pay me, I offer my gems of enlightenment without the motive of personal gain, I seek only to enrich all lives by sharing the rich and noble path that I have chosen.

I played Bingo for a bit today at a local hall, had an argument with the caller who refused to use the accepted pre-number phrases opting instead for topical pro-war puns -

"Drop that bomb - Twenty One"

"Support the War - Number Four"

"Watch that Landmine - Thirty Nine"

"Way to go Mr Bush - Twenty Eight"

Aside from supporting all this death and war, it made it impossible to pre-empt the numbers and optimise my marking off.

WEEK 9 DAY 6

Packed my bags and hit the road again this morning, I'm near to entering Pickens County now, the countryside here is beautiful, not as lovely as Shropshire, but stunning in its own way. Country Life would probably give it one out of ten.

The sunrise this morning over the cotton fields made me homesick for the simple pleasures of life in Moreton Say. I miss the quiet pace of life there, the lengthy conversations with old Mrs Randall about her wide-ranging and exotic medical problems, the familiar symphony of Mother and Aunt Felicity arguing about which low-fat spread was superior, lazy afternoons watching Countdown with a calculator, a dictionary and some cheese.

A couple driving an enormous camper van have picked me up. A lovely couple called Roland and Uma. Uma looks like an overweight Bette Davis and Roland bears a quite uncanny resemblance to Stewart Kidder, only without the wooden leg. They tell me they spend their retirement travelling the States and are more than happy for me to join them for as long as I like, my faith in human nature is restored.

They call their camper van a "Winnebago"; it has a wide screen TV, kitchen, shower, lounge and even a guest room. It's like a house on wheels, only nicer. They also have some sort of lizard living in there, like a pet that roams free. I'm not sure what sort of lizard it is, but I do know it's called Murray.

WEEK 9 DAY 7

I slept in the Winnebago's guest room, very cosy. The only thing that stopped me having a perfectly good night's sleep was the enormous portrait of Roland and Uma on the wall; they are both naked and riding unicorns. I say 'naked', they both have hardhats on. That isn't a euphemism. Yellow, plastic, hardhats.

Roland and Uma are incredibly hospitable, I stayed up late last night, past 11 o'clock, talking to them about Shropshire and my goal to tell the world about how marvellous it is there while at the same time righting wrongs and freeing the oppressed masses. They seemed genuinely interested, a response I am not accustomed to.

Today Uma is driving leaving Roland free to 'surf', which apparently is one of Roland's favourite things. He strips to his Y-Fronts, stands on the roof of the Winnebago on a small platform constructed especially for this purpose, straps his feet to the platform, smears himself in grease (to protect from the cold) and puts on his 'magic hat'. His hat looks to me like an industrial hardhat with the word "Happy" crayoned all over it, but Roland insists it is, in fact, a family heirloom and of great mystical importance. Then Uma puts her foot down and Roland spends the day waving at passing motorists and causing minor road accidents. I find it all very exhilarating and I'm not the one strapped to the top of a speeding Winnebago.

While Roland rode up top, I spoke to Uma as she drove. Uma tells me she is 107 years old, I'm not sure I believe her.

I'm going to try 'surfing' now, Roland is letting me wear his special hat.

Wish me luck

WEEK 10 DAY 1

Can't type today. Too much pain.

WEEK 10 DAY 2

I am slowly regaining use of my hands. It hurts to type but I know you all rely on me so I shall soldier on.

I neglected to apply protective grease before strapping myself to the roof of the Winnebago for a 'surf'. This proved to be a mistake. Uma kept on driving for six hours, unable to hear my screams for the Death Metal tape playing at full volume. By the time they pulled over I had passed out from exposure to the elements. I awoke with no sensation of any kind from the neck down and drool frozen to my cheek, a droolcicle.

Roland tells me that I passed out because the 'magic hat' rejected my aura.

I remember him saying - "If you're not in tune with the hat, the hat will know, man. You've gotta believe in the hat."

I used what little strength I had left to shout at Roland and Uma and tell them my condition was probably less to do with a magic hat rejecting me and more to do with being strapped half-naked to the top of a speeding vehicle for six hours by two mad old hippies. They promised to get me some help and left me lying on the floor of the Winnebago with Murray's vivarium lamp thawing me out, and then I nearly suffocated because Murray sat on my face to keep himself warm.

They dropped me off at a hospital.

I'm still there

Tubes are sticking out of me and I'm hooked up to a machine that beeps. The nurse jokingly said if it stops beeping then I'm dead, I didn't find that very funny.

WEEK 10 DAY 3

I feel bad about shouting at Roland and Uma. They were following their dream and I liked them for it. It's made me realise that one person's idea of utopia is not necessarily the same as another person's.

I think I know why this is.

Roland and Uma spent their lives trying to attain a state of constant pleasure. Having never been to Shropshire and experienced the fulfillment inherent in living there, they stumbled blindly for many years, trying various mystic disciplines before committing to the 'magic hat' thing. Now a lot of people are in the same condition as Roland and Uma, they know that they have a need but don't recognise that yearning for deeper satisfaction for what it is. Instead they mistake it for something less tangible and start messing around with dream catchers, crystals, magnetic fields and magic hats when all they really need to do is visit the West Midlands.

I firmly believe now that all people, no matter who they are or where they come from, have a genetic predisposition calling them to the soft bosom of Mother Shropshire. Perhaps it's because Shropshire is the only place where man has ever been truly happy; perhaps it's a homing instinct drawing them to something I don't understand, something mystical, something truly magical that only exists in Shropshire. Whatever it is, I know now more than ever that I need to educate people, stop them wasting time looking in the wrong places when all they want is waiting for them just down the M54.

I had a dream today, Shropshire rose up like a kindly giant, green and towering and smiling from a thousand lips. It grew and embraced the world, smothering it with love, pressing down joy and peace, holding tight until the goodness had suffused the whole world and there was nothing left but one continent, one people, one Shropshire. All the people of this new world did nothing but play Bingo and watch Countdown and were really, really nice to each other. Then Richard Whitely, King of the new world, made people do conundrums, even the ones who weren't very good at English and harshly punished the ones who couldn't guess the word in less than thirty seconds.

I think the painkillers I'm on are making me go a bit peculiar.

WEEK 10 DAY 4

I feel better today; I can feel my feet now. The nurse has been asking why I'm typing on my little palmtop and I explained about my life quest. She's called Alice and looks ever-so-slightly like Sebastian Newbold Coe, only with longer hair and a nurse's uniform and she's probably slower at running. I asked Alice if she had any suggestions for where I should travel next, she told me I wouldn't be going anywhere for a while yet.

I need inspiration, I need a sign.

A male nurse, Barry, came and saw me just now, I asked him about leaving and apparently I can discharge myself if I want, but they advise against it.

WEEK 10 DAY 5

The nurse, her surname apparently is Springs – Alice Springs. I think that this may be some sort of sign. I asked Barry what his surname was too - It's Areef – Barry Areef.

That's good enough for me, my mind is made up, and as soon as I can I'm flying to Australia.
If Shropshire really does exude a supernatural aura of goodness, then surely the people most in need of my help are those furthest away from it's positive powers, and geographically Australia is as far away from Shropshire as you can get without going into orbit.

After a minor skirmish with hospital security, I've discharged myself and feel absolutely fine, though I do still have a couple of clear plastic tubes sticking out of my arm. My flight to Alice Springs leaves tonight, goodbye America, g'day Australia.

WEEK 10 DAY 6

I'm on the plane. It's quite a long flight.

The in-flight movie is "Daredevil", it's an action/special effects extravaganza about a blind lawyer who gains superpowers after getting covered in radioactive fluid, it's not as good as "Gone To Earth".

WEEK 10 DAY 7

I'm still on the plane, we landed somewhere for a while but we were not allowed to get off the plane. I change planes once more before we land at Alice Springs airport.

There's some turbulence, the woman sat next to me has woken up and is panicking, I comfort her with tales of Shropshire, and she quickly falls asleep again.

I've landed, the great outback stretches out before me, and I'm as far away from Shropshire now as I can physically be. My beloved Moreton Say is now on the other side of the planet and the barren wilds of Australia await my compassionate touch and nurture. I have extensive knowledge of Australia, it's people and customs, having studied Neighbours and Home And Away for many years, so I feel fully equipped to deal with anything Oz might throw at me.

It's very, very hot here. I buy a thermos to keep my bingo markers cool in, they were beginning to melt.

I hope I do better here than I did in America.

WEEK 11 DAY 1

My first full day in Australia, it's not at all like Neighbours. The people seem very laid back and friendly, more like Paul Hogan than Harold or Lou. The airport was packed and I declined the numerous offers to take my bag, it surprises me how many people who seem perfectly capable of carrying their own luggage trust a complete stranger to run off with it the minute they get off the plane.

I'm getting the bus into the city of Alice Springs from the airport; it's a few miles away. After such a long flight, I'm as tired as the Moreton Say roof thatcher the day after it rained frogs and I'm going to check into a hotel to gather my thoughts before I tackle my antipodean brethren.

Alice Springs, immortalised by Peter Finch and Virginia McKenna in the 1956 classic "A Town Like Alice", actually looks a bit bleak, a lot of sand, very dry, and disappointingly I have yet to see one person wearing a hat with corks dangling from it or playing a didgeridoo. I'm staying at the Heavitree Gap Outback Lodge which is actually very nice, my room has a kitchen and a fridge and there are wallabies you can feed. I tried to feed one of the wallabies, I'm not sure what wallabies eat but they don't seem very keen on my Kendal Mint Cake.

I've been doing some research on Alice Springs, primarily by reading the free leaflets in my room. Ayers rock is quite near and a place of great mystical importance so I might go there and see if it compares to Shropshire's famous mystical centrepoint -The Wrekin.

WEEK 11 DAY 2

Eager to make an impact early on, I shuttlebussed into Alice Springs today and started talking to as many people as I could.

I met a lot of backpackers.

Found a cyber-café called "Byte-Me" and set up a temporary base of operations.

I searched the local newsagents for copies of "Country Life", thankfully their poison does not seem to have reached Australia yet so I won't have to combat any Shropshire misinformation among the locals of Alice Springs. I have yet to have a reply from Country Life about their so-called survey that placed Shropshire 20th out of 37 English counties despite many Emails to them demanding a recount.

I'd encourage all like-minded Shropshire lovers to Email Country Life's 'News Editor' and ask her for a written apology, let me know if you hear from her.

A group of backpackers from Sydney seemed very interested in my recollections of Shropshire village life. They are five girls – Cherry, Brittany, Kylie, Chelsea and Amy. Brittany seemed particularly impressed when I told her I had seen Crocodile Dundee eleven times. They set off for Ayers rock in four days and I have arranged to join them. All five of them seem very nice and have minds open to new ideas. I hope to convince them all to relocate to Shropshire, perhaps one of them could get to know Toby.

Chelsea has a tattoo of Rolf Harris on her lower back, it's very tasteful.

I also met a man called Grub who paints Australian wildlife using his own bodily fluids.

WEEK 11 DAY 3

I bought some supplies for my planned trek to Ayers rock, chocolate and crisps mostly.

Today I met a man called Gregory who looked like a young John Wayne with bad teeth. Gregory had a disturbing background. He was from Market Drayton. He had forsaken the perfect homeland for the Australian outback, not to embark on some noble quest to enlighten, but to chase money in some greedy misguided notion that being rich materially was better than being enriched by living in Shropshire. He left eleven years ago and has never returned, despite the fact that he could have boarded a plane at any time and once again drank from the crystal streams of joy and goodness waiting for him on the other side of the world in his home county.

His story deeply shocked me, more so when Gregory revealed he had no plans to return to Shropshire, ever. I showed him some postcards of home, I did some impressions of Shropshire wildlife, I made him smell the Tupperware container full of Shropshire earth that I carry at all times in case of emergency, I even offered to buy him a ticket home and he laughed, nothing could rekindle a desire to see Shropshire once more. He told me he owns a successful business, has a nice house, happy family, three cars and "prefers it here".

I did the only thing I could, I paid a local thug (a lovely man called Terry, seven feet tall with one ear and a lisp) to kidnap him, render him unconscious and get him on the first flight back to England. He'll thank me when he wakes up.

WEEK 11 DAY 4

Mother rang today, everything is fine at home. I asked after Toby and Sophia, Mother said she hasn't seen much of them since Toby moved out of our house and into next door. I can only presume Toby is working long hours and Mother doesn't see him come and go. The curtains are drawn night and day, which seems odd; perhaps Sophia is developing film in her living room. I tried to ring Toby at work and they said he wasn't there. I hope everything is alright, I wanted to tell Toby about the girls I've met.

I walked around Alice Springs today, I saw not one spring and met no-one called Alice. I did meet a woman called Rita, she was only four feet tall and was wearing one of those hats with corks dangling off it. Finally.

WEEK 11 DAY 5

It's still very hot here. I'm resting today in my room, my last day of comfort before I join the girls.

Today I've been reading some of the comments left for me on the BBC message board. Thankyou to everyone for taking such an interest, I'm sorry I can't reply personally to everyone but I'm very busy saving the world.

It's always a pleasure to hear from the other Mike Batt who points out that 'Tarka the Otter' and 'Sense and Sensibility' were both filmed in Devon and "take advantage of Devon's award winning countryside". I've seen both those films and distinctly remember that when I watched them I thought "that countryside isn't half as nice as Moreton Say".

James the Shropshire Lad suggests I kick something out of whoever said Shropshire was the worst place to live. While I understand your anger James, it is always best to put such strong feelings to a non-violent use. Violence is like Richard Whitely, it never solves problems, it only creates them. As Melvin Bone quite rightly points out "kicking the *s%!t* out of whoever did the poll is not really going with Morris philosophy on life".

Clive Bevan helpfully points out the usefulness of the Weetabix Book of Survival, I'll keep an eye out for it.

The Mailman from Perth gave me some extremely exciting information, apparently Perth is home to "the biggest bingo hall in the Southern Hemisphere". I was initially unsure where to head from Alice Springs, now my destination is Perth and the tantalisingly named "biggest bingo", I can't wait. Apparently Perth is 2,000 kilometres away, so it might take quite a while if I hitchhike, but I sense it will be worth every minute.

The hotel has air-conditioning that seems to consist of a large box in the corner of my room that keeps me awake with a variety of unusual whirring, clanking and grinding noises without actually producing any cool air. I slept with my head in the fridge.

WEEK 11 DAY 6

I met Cherry, Brittany, Kylie, Chelsea and Amy at Byte Me this morning and we are all setting off for Ayers Rock. We could just get a bus but instead we are hiking across the outback.

Apparently the girls are an all-female Beatles tribute band, except for Kylie who's an accountant. They sang "Paperback Writer" as we walked, expect for Kylie and Amy. Amy is Ringo.

It's very hot.

WEEK 11 DAY 7

We are not as well prepared as we might be for trekking across desert terrain, we are low on water already. The girls noticed my Thermos and asked what I had in it, I had a difficult time explaining why it was full of bingo markers. Brittany is map reading; I don't like the way she keeps turning the map around trying to work out which way up it goes.

An Aboriginal man approached us as we walked. He also seemed very interested in my tales of Shropshire life. After talking about myself for a few hours, I left him with a postcard of Oswestry and forty Australian dollars; he in turn gave me a boomerang. It was a moment of great cultural understanding and exchange, though I was a little disappointed when I noticed the boomerang was made of plastic and manufactured in China. Cherry showed me how to throw the boomerang, it comes back to you when you throw it, I prefer yo-yos.

I'm uncomfortably hot, the girls are keeping up quite a pace and I am struggling to keep up and type on my palmtop at the same time. I was hoping we might be able to see Ayers Rock by now, but all I can see for miles is flat, featureless desert, as flat and featureless as a fresh sheet of A3. I'm beginning to wonder if knowing the lyrics to the entire Beatles back catalogue qualifies you to navigate desert terrain.

WEEK 12 DAY 1

We probably should have done more preparation before walking into the Outback. I may have exaggerated my survival expertise when I was chatting to Cherry, Brittany, Kylie, Chelsea and Amy in Alice Springs. Now I think about it, it was shortly after I told them I was Ray Mears brother that they asked if I'd like to join them.

My lips are cracked and dry like one of Mother's homemade biscuits only without the smiley face made out of icing.

The five girls I am travelling with are struggling too; they started hallucinating this morning, the four girls from the Beatles tribute band started thinking they really were John, Paul, George and Ringo. Kylie, the accountant, then started shouting at the sky saying she was Jon Bon Jovi and demanding someone bring her some celery and a hairdryer. I'm new to Australian social situations but I suspect this is not normal behaviour.

I know who I am.

I am Morris Telford and I shall prevail.

WEEK 12 DAY 2

The flying doctor arrived just two hours after I called him. John had started to call me Yoko so he arrived just in time.

I'm in hospital again, I hope this doesn't become a theme of my travels. Oddly, the Nurse here is called Margaret Drayton.

WEEK 12 DAY 3

I've been told I'm not allowed to use my palmtop and phone in the hospital so I might not be able to update much for a few days. I have to borrow a white coat and sneak into the hospital garden to type entries and keep getting disturbed by in-patients who think I'm a doctor.

I've cured three people just while typing this.

WEEK 12 DAY 4

Looked in the hospital library for the Weetabix Book of Survival, no sign of it anywhere.

WEEK 12 DAY 5

They have increased the anti-psychotics the girls are on. Kylie no longer thinks she is Jon Bon Jovi, she now thinks she is Sue Pollard. A definite improvement.

WEEK 12 DAY 6

I think they will let us go soon. After some minor encouragement from me, the four Beatle girls tried to stage a concert on the hospital roof, but the structure was unsound and they fell through the ceiling halfway through Strawberry Fields and landed on an elderly man in intensive care. Kylie came to the rescue and carried him to safety shouting "Hi-De-Hi!".

The blows to the head that the girls suffered as they fell seems to have done the trick and they are once again coherent, lucid and ready to follow my lead.

WEEK 12 DAY 7

They let us out, I feel much better now.

My experience in the Australian outback would be the sort of thing that might put a lot of people off, but I do not balk from a challenge, I shall not let the elements beat me. I am setting off right now for Ayers Rock with the girls; I convinced them we must face our demons.

To be fair, we are taking a bus this time.

Sat on the bus, I've been reading the BBC message board.

A big thanks to Melvin Bone for all the Australian travel advice. Unfortunately by the time I read about Alice Springs being hundreds of miles from Ayers Rock it was a bit late. Though apparently when the flying doctors picked us up we were actually further from Ayers Rock than Alice Springs is, if there's one thing I have learned in Australia, it is never trust a Ringo Starr impersonator to map-read for you.

The "One spider lives under toilet seats and has the venom to kill a horse" comment confused me, if it lives under a toilet seat how did it end up biting a horse? Was it the seat of a horse's toilet?

I also take exception to this - "Devon looks three times as nice as in Tarka the Otter making it 50% better than Shropshire by your own reckonings". If you think Devon is actually three times nicer than it looks in Tarka the Otter, then I must have only enjoyed Tarka the Otter one eighth as much as most people and if you only enjoyed it half as much as me then that makes Shropshire at least four times better than Devon by anyone's calculations.

I can see Ayers Rock in the distance now. It looks a bit bigger than The Wrekin.

WEEK 13 DAY 1

Finally, Ayers Rock stands before me. It rises majestically from the outback like a cake. A giant, brown, mystical rock cake with clouds for icing, tourists and kangaroos scattered around it for hundreds and thousands, and Australia for a serving plate. I can't see anything big enough to suffice as a knife, though you could separate the roofs of Sydney Opera house and use them as makeshift spoons.

Last night we were encouraged to sleep in the open to allow the rock to speak to us in our dreams. I also ate some cheese just before bedtime to enhance the effect and soon after I dreamt about walking down the streets of my beloved Moreton Say. It was so vivid I could smell the spring blossoms, hear the lilting birdsong and taste the Twix I had bought at Mr Pollocks corner shop. It was truly magical and when I awoke my resolve to spread the Moreton Say message was diamond hard.

Cherry, Brittany, Kylie, Chelsea and Amy told me they all dreamed of walking through the most beautiful place they had ever seen. It was full of colour and joy, populated by people both generous and happy, where the animals and birds were tame and content, the water was crystal clear and tasted of liquid laughter, and the air itself sang with music that made them weep with fulfilment. So essentially the same dream as mine, but without the Twix.

They took a little bit of convincing that there dream was also about Moreton Say, but after I talked to them for several hours in the extreme heat they all agreed that it must have been Shropshire they saw in their dream.

Chelsea promised to have a map of Shropshire tattooed over her Rolf Harris and all five girls made a solemn vow there and then to tell others of their awakening to the wonder that is Shropshire. They each had tears in their eyes as they left me just now to follow their own destinies as the sun set over the big cake of Ayers Rock. They wanted to stay with me, become my followers but I had to explain that the path I have chosen is one I must walk alone. Mostly.

WEEK 13 DAY 2

The unforgiving Australian sun has finally had it's evil way with my Bingo markers. Despite keeping them cool in a thermos, they are melted beyond all recognition. It's probably for the best, I know I should not put such value on material possessions. Anyway, when I reach Perth, home of Australia's biggest bingo hall, I'm sure I can replace them.

Despite specific advice to the contrary, I am trusting my instincts and trying to hitchhike my way to Perth. It's been a few days since I had any major life-threatening experiences so now the girls have left I thought I'd strike out on my own again for a while and enjoy the full-on Australian outback experience.

I called home and spoke to Mother but the line was terrible. She asked where I was and when she heard me say "Outback" there was a thump and the line went quiet. A few minutes later Aunt Felicity came on the line and explained that Mother was in our back garden looking for me, screaming my name at the herbaceous borders, I left her to explain to Mother all about Australia.

WEEK 13 DAY 3

Walking in Oz is slow progress, I can still see Ayers Rock behind me. It's hot, really hot. The sun feels like it is slapping the back of my head every few seconds, I now know what people mean when they say the sun is beating down on them. Yet again my Ordinance Survey map of Shropshire is proving invaluable, it acts as an excellent sunshield.

I met a camera crew today, they were filming a news item about the dangers of the inhospitable outback, so I think I rather spoiled things for them when I walked up with a map tied to my head.

I offered my help to them. I have had some limited experience of television production, I'm an avid watcher of Countdown and often read the credits at the end of the programme. I was once nearly a contestant on Fifteen-To-One, my general knowledge is excellent but only if the question is Shropshire related, so I didn't ring the application hotline. I explained this to the people filming and told them all about Moreton Say and the delights therein. They seemed mildly interested and filmed a short piece about me, I hope it gets broadcast, I did notice that the presenter started his item about me with "and finally". They were also kind enough to offer me a ride, but it's such a lovely sunny day it seemed a shame not to walk.

I'm setting up my little tent now. A very large spider just walked past, it was like a big hairy melon with eight legs and an attitude, I hid behind a rock until it was gone. Unfortunately the rock I hid behind seemed to be the home of a large snake that I inadvertently stood on. I apologised to the snake but it tried to bite me nonetheless. Fortunately my Ordinance Survey map of Shropshire acted as a protective shield and I was able to escape injury. Looking at the map later, the snake had left two small but visible holes with it's fangs on either side of Oswestry. It made me wonder if the snake had some deep-seated reptilian longing for Shropshire too and wasn't actually attacking me, but just marking a place on the map it fancied visiting, if indeed all creatures long to live there but like so many humans are denied by the cruel geographical lottery of birth.

WEEK 13 DAY 4

I'm having a little difficulty keeping going in this heat. I thought that without the extra burden of looking after John, Paul, George, Ringo and Jon Bon Jovi I would be managing fine, I may have been overly optimistic. Since my quest is to tell as many as possible about Shropshire and help solve problems and right wrongs, it has occurred to me that an uninhabitable desert is not the very best place to meet people and fulfill these goals.

Shockingly, I just came across some bleached human bones on a rock outcropping. The poor soul had been picked clean by whatever picks things clean in Australia. All that remains are the bleached bones, the ragged remains of a bag and a self-help book "How to Survive the Australian Outback". It's not a terribly good advertisement for the book. I once read "How To Make Friends and Influence People", it didn't mention Shropshire once.

Civilisation at last! I've reached a small outback town. I say town, it has four sheds, a bar, a petrol station and an outside lavatory. I'm going for a drink of water at the bar.

WEEK 13 DAY 5

I stayed at the bar last night. It's called "The Filthy Mug" and is owned and run by a lovely old lady called Margaret with the most prominent ears I have ever seen. Margaret looks like Yoda, only taller and less green. When she walks through a door she has to turn slightly or her ears brush against the doorframe. Oddly, her hearing is terrible.

The four sheds I saw yesterday, corrugated iron lean-tos, are actually houses. I've only met one of the occupants so far, he lives in the shed nearest the Filthy Mug and his name, as far as I can gather, is Meat. He has hair down to his ankles, wide staring eyes and seems to be wearing a loincloth. He seems very nice.

It's difficult getting much sense out of Margaret; she doesn't seem to know where Meat comes from or what his real name is. He just comes into the bar every night and sits on the floor saying "Meat, meat, meat" until Margaret throws him a burger. I saw him do this last night, he eats the burger and then goes back to his shed. It's not much of a life but he seems quite happy. I asked Meat if he wanted to come with me, but all he did was keep saying "Meat" again and again. So I gave him my spare shirt and a postcard with a picture of Market Drayton to enhance his lifestyle and give him a little taste of Shropshire. Maybe he will look at the postcard long enough to develop a healthy yearning for Shropshire and one day try to improve himself and travel there.

Margaret is letting me stay at the Filthy Mug again tonight, then its back on the road.

WEEK 13 DAY 6

I've decided Perth is much too far away to walk. My feet hurt and I long for the simple pleasures, a soft bed, a nice cup of tea and a game of Bingo. I can see something on the horizon to the north; a flat topped mountain or something so I'm heading for that.

Still very hot.

I'm getting nearer the mountain, the nearer I get the more it looks like Ayers Rock, I didn't realise there was more than one of them.

WEEK 13 DAY 7

I reached the mountain, I found out why it looks so much like Ayers Rock. It is Ayers Rock. I must have been walking in a big circle, it's very difficult to find your way round the Australian outback, it all looks the same. In Moreton Say I never got lost. In Moreton Say you are never far from a familiar landmark, you can trace your journey on an Ordinance Survey map and there are no snakes, spiders or kangaroos, the most dangerous animal you might meet is Farmer Henshaw's dog, Walnut.

There's a very interesting reason behind why the dog was called Walnut, but I can't for the life of me remember what it is.

I'm getting a bus back to Alice Springs and from there I'm going to fly to Perth. I see no reason why I can't combine my mission of justice with a little recreation, so I'm going to find "Biggest Bingo" and see how Australia's premier Bingo Hall compares with Sunday night at Market Drayton.

I'm stopping at "Byte Me", the Internet Café to check the message board. Thankyou to everyone for the messages of support they have left. Knowing that my simple words are educating people all over the world about the wonders Shropshire has to offer are a great motivation for me.

I notice that Australia is compared to Telford Town Park by John Rowe. Obviously there is no real comparison, that 180 hectares of wildlands in the heart of Telford make the Australian outback look like a child's sandpit. For those of you who have not sampled the dark delights of Telford Town Park, it's a place of whispers and frenzy, shady woodlands and ancient secrets. By day little children play on the Giant Spider's Web, the Rocket Slide, the Wooden Adventure Area or pedal a boat across Southwater Lake. By night the old men gather on the bandstand and tell tales of the sundial made from human collarbones and the network of tunnels that lay underneath the park and date back to a time before human speech.

Thankyou to Catherine for remembering my birthday, with each passing year I grow to love and appreciate Shropshire that little bit more.

Kazakhstan, Iraq and Singapore are all suggested as my next destination. I'm not sure where my path leads after Oz. I go where the winds of fate take me, wherever the desperate cry of the needy can be heard, wherever persecution casts it's shadow, wherever people are ignorant of Shropshire and all it has to offer, and wherever you can play an honest game of Bingo in hygienic surroundings.

WEEK 14 DAY 1

I've just arrived in the city of Perth, Western Australia. It's very nice. It's no Telford, but it's very nice.

A message left for me by 'M' said about Perth -

"You will also be glad to find the biggest bingo hall in the Southern Hemisphere there, aptly called 'Biggest Bingo'.

I've already asked a few people if they know where "Biggest Bingo", the Southern Hemispheres largest Bingo emporium is. No one seems to know.

WEEK 14 DAY 2

I am spending today trying to meet the people of Perth and get a feel for their wants and needs. Each place I visit has a distinct personality. So far most of the places I have travelled outside Shropshire seem to have dysfunctional personalities. Except possibly for Tuscaloosa, who was just a bit confused.

Where Ludlow might strike you as an old gentleman with a face worn by hardship and happiness, Perth seems to me more like a young man just out of his teens, full of half-realised opportunities, wary of over-stretching himself, possibly a Mark 3 Ford Capri driver, with short blonde hair, one of those thin little goatee beards like Beppe di Marco in Eastenders and a slight squint in the left eye.

I've booked into a hotel and I am now going down to a place called Barrack Square that is apparently a good place to meet people. The square is square shaped, with a group of palm trees near the middle where people congregate.

I got talking to a group of students that were on some sort of field trip. Bizarrely, it seems that the schools here don't teach very much at all about Shropshire, instead they concentrate their time on Australian history and culture. I asked them if they knew where Biggest Bingo was, they didn't. Very disappointing.

I also met a young lady called Susan today who looked just like Mother Teresa, only younger and without the tea towel. Susan works in the noble profession of obtaining, maintaining and distributing office consumables. We talked paperclips and laser printer toner cartridges for the best part of the day and I could feel a real connection between us, I asked her if she wanted to leave her life as an office supplies operative and embark on a journey of self-discovery and Shropshire related promotion activities.

She said "no".

I understood her reaction. The sweet and heady allure of the paperclip order-form can be a difficult mistress to forsake. I left her with directions to Moreton Say in case she changes her mind.

Meeting Susan made me think of my previous life in Mr Magson's department. Not once have I regretted quitting my job and devoting my life to enriching the world, but I'd be lying if I said I didn't occasionally miss that rush of blood to the head you get when the new quarterly stationary catalogue is delivered.

WEEK 14 DAY 3

Walked around Perth. No sign of Biggest Bingo anywhere. I found the beach, miles of golden sands and clear blue sea, but not one donkey ride or stick of rock.

WEEK 14 DAY 4

Toby rang me, he sounded very happy. Apparently his relationship with Sophia, my old next-door neighbour and object of my admiration, has blossomed over the past few weeks and they are getting engaged.

I think Toby looks up to me as a mentor and guide, so I naturally warned him about the dangers of rushing into these things. It was while I was warning him that he dropped another bombshell.

Sophia is pregnant.

I'm not quite sure how this all happened, but Toby seems quite convinced it is his child she carries. I lived next door to Sophia for decades and the most contact I ever had was cleaning leaves out of her gutters while she was out. Toby only met her a few weeks ago and not only has he impregnated Sophia, apparently he fitted a new downpipe last week too.

I'm very happy for them both.

WEEK 14 DAY 5

I don't feel like I've been having the impact in Perth that I should be having.

I need to get people's attention and make them realise that they are wasting their time in the blazing Australian sunshine when they could be shopping at the Market Drayton village hall, visiting the many places of historical interest or walking the gentle slopes of Shropshire's fine countryside.

I'm thinking I'm going to stage a Salopian event.

I just can't decide what sort of event.

WEEK 14 DAY 6

I met a man today who spends part of his year organising whistle stop tours of Britain.

The sort of tour where they cram 64 American Tourists into a coach and spend a week driving around Britain at the end of which they think they have "seen" Great Britain.

They stop at notable locations, bundle them out of the coach for a half-hour look round and then move on to the next location.

I think I eventually convinced him that all real British achievement stems in one way or another from Shropshire.

After several hours of persuading and a few hundred dollars he agreed to stop wasting all that time at Shakespeare's House and Tower Bridge and spend seven days camped at Ironbridge instead.

Another triumph for common sense.

WEEK 14 DAY 7

I've decided on an event to stage here. It will shatter the public consciousness and awaken the good people of Perth to the infinite possibilities of life in Shropshire. I'm going to have an auction.

I've booked a local MC, a small portable stage and some girls in bikinis. Tomorrow I am going to set up in the middle of Barrack Square, auction some of my Shropshire related belongings (some postcards, some polaroids of Moreton Say signed by me, a snowstorm from a shop in Oswestry, my sunglasses I wore while in Shropshire and a packet of spearmints Polos I bought at my local shop and had forgotten about) and then as a final grand gesture, I am auctioning myself.

Whoever loves Shropshire enough to bid the most for me will get Morris Telford's exclusive services for three whole days and nights.

I've put some flyers around the city.

I expect a big crowd.

I might ask them if anyone knows where Biggest Bingo is.

WEEK 15 DAY 1

It's very early morning and quite blustery today in Perth, not an ill wind of change but a friendly, warm breeze of opportunity, the sort that would be really good for drying clothes in, not big, thick wool clothes obviously but excellent for cotton, nylon and socks.

Barrack Square is getting ready for a full-on auction of Salopian memorabilia. Up for grabs are some signed (by me) postcards and polaroids of Moreton Say, a little snowstorm from Oswestry, my sunglasses, a packet of Polos (I bought them in Shropshire but I'd be the first to admit the link is tenuous) and me.

The stage platform is being set up and the MC I hired has just arrived.

I hadn't met the MC before now and it seems to me his advert was a little misleading. I booked "Crazy Mick - Perth's most dynamic, bombastic, happening master of ceremonies. Perfect for all your major events, receptions, auctions, parties and functions. "
Crazy Mick's real name is Cyril who looks a little bit like David Dickinson might if he really let himself go. He is mahogany, 53, overweight, balding and admits this is his first ever gig. He does look the part in his mauve rhinestone jump-suit though.

Mick is auctioning the snowstorm now. It would be an exaggeration to say that things are going spectacularly well. No one has actually bid on anything yet, the postcards and polaroids failed to fire up the enthusiasm of any bargain hunters, though a small crowd has gathered.

Someone just bought the snowstorm, there was a minor bidding war, one man bid $1, then someone else bid $1.50, then the first man came back with a bid of $1.75 which proved too rich for the other bidder and won the auction. Exciting stuff.

Things are really hotting up now, the Polos attracted seven bids and finished at $18.00, they must be hard to get hold of here or something. I hope no one notices I ate one and folded the silver foil back over. I'm up for auction next, whoever wins gets my exclusive services for three whole days and nights, I hope someone nice wins.

I'm a bit nervous now; Crazy Mick just introduced me as "a lot for the ladies, Shropshire's answer to Mel Gibson, the original Crocodile hunter, Morris Telford." I have to go now and sell myself.

WEEK 15 DAY 2

This is the first time I've had chance to type anything since the auction ended.

I am, apparently, worth $17.50

$17.50 for three days and three nights of Morris Telford. I wouldn't mind so much, but the Polos sold for more than I did.

Still, fate has once again smiled on me, the auction was won by a man called Chip Roland who looks a bit like an young Todd Carty, just after he left Grange Hill but before he got Aids. Chip owns a stationary supplies company ("Chip's Clips, Paper and Staplers, Perth WA") and I am once again up to my elbows in office paraphernalia, no one could be happier at such a fortuitous outcome. Except possibly Chip who has employed an experienced office consumables clerk for less than six dollars a day.

I started yesterday morning and immediately set about reorganising the stock allocation and ordering process so that it conforms to a more modern, indexed system. I felt almost guilty enjoying it so much, sat surrounded by box upon box of poorly organised stationary supplies, it's like a little holiday. Would you believe I actually found a box of the pre-code banner twist file ringlets?

After work finished at seven, Chip took me home with him. On reflection I was leaving myself open for abuse by pledging 24-hour days, but I'm a man of my word so I went home with Chip and it wasn't so bad. He did make me wear a giant teddy bear suit and kept me up most of the night making me sing Waltzing Matilda while he stapled pictures of his ex-wife to the furniture. Chip cried himself to sleep at about 6am so I left him to sleep and got back to work at the stationary suppliers. I changed out of the teddy suit first.

Today is day 100 of my Salopian Opus. A centenary of sacrifice, a milestone of personal triumph and a red-letter day for all lovers of Shropshire. I suspect the streets of Moreton Say are ringing with the cries of rejoicing and celebration, that's probably why no-one answered when I called home, they are all busy doing parades and waving flags and things like that.

The postcards and polaroids that didn't sell at auction are being put to good use; I'm slipping one into each order that is dispatched from Chip's company, spreading a little Shropshire goodness along with the paperclips.

When I worked for Mr Magson I used to put signed photos of myself in any stationary orders I was particularly proud of but he made me stop it. No one appreciates professional pride anymore.

I'll have to stop typing, Chip has arrived.

WEEK 15 DAY 3

Last night after work, Chip made me paint his house, unblock his drains and cut his hair.

He opened up a bit while I cut his hair, apparently his wife Sheila left him last year and he never really got over it. He seemed to love her very much.

I had a long chat with him, tried to explain to him how important it is to move on, start a new chapter of his life, perhaps move to Shropshire, I think it really helped him having someone to talk to. After I cut his hair he made me wear one of Sheila's old dresses while I read to him. He couldn't decide what he wanted me to read, so I chose the 2003 Stationary Supplies Catalogue of Western Australia and read through the pages of new stock items. Chip fell asleep about halfway through the desk diaries on page 57, but I kept on reading anyway until the sun came up.

This morning I changed back into my own clothes while Chip slept on and opened the business up for him. He called me just now and thanked me, it's the first full night's sleep he has had since his wife left. I hope Chip will be able to cope without me.

WEEK 15 DAY 4

Last night was my last night of auction servitude, I've not had much sleep for three days and I'm going to check into a hotel and rest.

I have left Chip's stationary business in better order than it has ever been, I'm not sure that Chip himself is much better though. I kept telling him that if he only relocated to Shropshire he would be much happier, he was foolishly sceptical about moving to Shropshire being a panacea, how little he knows of the deep happiness you enjoy just by being in England's finest county (Shropshire, not Devon).

He is deeply unhappy and uses the business as an excuse for staying as he is, I'm very worried about him.

Things actually got a bit out of hand last night with Chip, suffice to say I had to use an industrial staple gun to protect my virtue. I shan't be auctioning myself again.

WEEK 15 DAY 5

I've just seen this on the Morris Telford BBC messageboard -

"I am sure that your feet will be thanking you for every step in your pilgrimage towards the Holy Grail of bingo halls, on golden sands of beautiful Perth. The address of The Biggest Bingo Centre is 496 Guildford Rd Bayswater...I only hope this message reaches you in time. "

Hurrah! Today I shall play Bingo like never before.

The Biggest Bingo Centre stands on Guildford Rd like a radiant bastion of pure joy. Inside the air is thick with warm love and the nostril-arousing aroma of freshly opened bingo markers. After the past few days I think I deserve a little self-indulgence, I intend to play until my arms go numb and my eyes bleed.

Contrary to popular opinion, Bingo, like life, is not about winning; it's all about the journey. The chair you sit in, the tone and performance of the caller, the marker you use, the type of grid your numbers are in; any one of these factors can totally change the bingo playing experience.

The moment you walk into the Bingo Hall a galaxy of possibilities open up before you. Who will you sit next to? How many cards will you play simultaneously? What colour maker will you use? Is the method used to select the numbers a genuinely random system? Can you hold out to the end of the game before going to the toilet? All these exciting forks in the Bingo road are just as important as "will I win?"

In saying all this, I did scream like a banshee when I won $132,568.28 just now in the national game. Bingo, like life, rewards people at random.

WEEK 15 DAY 6

I've put my winnings to good use, I've bought Chip's Clips, Paper and Staplers, Perth WA. It's always been a dream of mine to own my own stationary company, and now I do. I gave Chip a one-way airline ticket to the UK and directions to my old home in Moreton Say, my bedroom is free now that Toby has moved in with Sophia and I'm sure Mother won't mind if Chip stays with her for a bit.

Today I hastily assembled a ragtag fleet of jobless, homeless and in a couple of cases hairless people to run the office supplies business for me. Once the twinkling magnificence of stationary ordering grabs them I'm sure the business will thrive in my absence.

I also called the Filthy Mug and I'm going to have Meat brought up to Perth to help run the business. Once he learns to speak I'm sure he will make an excellent stationary operative.

Much as I would like to settle here and run Morris Telford's Clips, Paper and Staplers, Perth WA, I have a greater calling to attend to and must once again forsake the lure of the paperclip.

My new team get to keep all the profits; the only stipulation I make is that all orders sent out have a free Ordinance Survey Map of Shropshire sent with them, with a little red ring around the location of Moreton Say. Soon every office in Western Australia will know where Moreton Say is.

WEEK 15 DAY 7

After my time with Chip I feel ready for a change, I've been thinking about where to go next and saw that Deuan Jones had been thinking about the same thing on the message board -

"I've been wondering where on earth Morris would go next - which part of the planet most needs his unique touch, which harbours the most urgent problems, and then I'm sure I spotted him the other day in Amsterdam! I do hope he deals with that dreadful 'dance music' everybody seems to be into here, and maybe takes home some of the embarrassing British who have defused over here!"

No, that wasn't me, I've never been to Amsterdam, it's not a bad idea though. I was thinking of going to Devon and proving to myself just how wrong Country Life really were, but if Amsterdam is where I am needed, then that is where I shall go. I'm very sorry to hear about the dance music and that some British people are being embarrassing, you have to remember that not all British people come from Shropshire. I'll pop over and see what I can do.

Do they speak English in Amsterdam? I do hope so. I'll admit I know absolutely nothing about Amsterdam. Except, of course, that it won't be half as nice as Shropshire.

My plane leaves tonight.

WEEK 16 DAY 1

As suggested by Deuan Jones, I'm on a plane, flying to Holland, land of tulips, clogs, windmills and cheese.

My plane lands at Amsterdam Airport in a few hours so I am spending the time wisely reading as much as I can about Amsterdam, its people, its culture and its travel system.

It all looks very interesting and a location ripe for an infusion of my special Shropshire blend of love and goodness.

I must admit that when I previously thought of Amsterdam it conjured up images of shop windows with no curtains, with an overweight leather-clad dominatrix on display in one and an emaciated scantily clad young lady in another, all with a hazy, unhappy atmosphere of mind-altering mist.

The brochures paint a different picture entirely; they talk of an Amsterdam rich in art and culture, teeming with a diverse tapestry of historical interest and "a city that overflows with architectural style". Perhaps I was confusing Amsterdam with Devon.

They play a lot of dance music in Amsterdam, every car that goes by seems to have it blaring out. While I try my best to embrace all cultures and lifestyles in my bid to understand why so many people choose not to live in Shropshire, I'm not a big fan of dance music.

It's very repetitive and always seems to be playing at too high a volume. It's not as bad as country music though. I hope no one ever comes up with dance-country music. That would be truly terrible.

The insipid lyrics and sentiment of Country combined with the incessant drumbeat of Dance. It would probably go straight to number one and then get banned when people died trying to line dance to it.

WEEK 16 DAY 2

I walked the streets of Amsterdam today, soaking in the atmosphere and seeing what injustices festered here that I could address.

I can sense a sadness in Amsterdam, a feeling around me that people are trying to cram in as much as they possibly can into the city, but ultimately they always fall short, they never quite reach that perfect blend of spirituality, physicality and emotional resonance that you feel the moment you set foot in somewhere like Oswestry or Ludlow.

You don't get this much loud music in Oswestry or Ludlow either. I haven't seen anything of the seedier side of Amsterdam.

My Mother called me and told me not to speak to any strange women so I hung up on her immediately.

WEEK 16, DAY 3

I met a man called Hans today. Hans looks like Jack Kirby drew him. He has a large head, a brow overhang that juts way over his eyebrows leaving his eyes in permanent shade, a thickset square jaw, wide mouth and hands like industrial shovels. He must have been inked by Vince Coletta though as his left thumb is missing.

Hans lives on a barge and from what I can gather, he makes his living by fishing rubbish out of the canal and selling it to tourists. He's very inventive, in the past few hours he has sold a Vauxhall wing mirror as an art-deco soap dish, what looked to me like a soggy old bit of cardboard as a vintage Roman doormat, a lump of driftwood saying it was one of the last remaining pieces of Amsterdam's once famous hand-carved pier, and a hubcap to a couple of Americans telling them it was a renaissance Frisbee.

I've spent most of the day talking to Hans, his English is not great, but better than that of some of the people I met in Birmingham, and he has had a fascinating life. He was sold into slavery as a young child and was raised at sea by pirates. When he grew too big to fit in a barrel (I didn't understand that bit either) he lived in the Paris sewers making a modest living shining shoes and cleaning windows. He saved enough money to buy a dinghy and once he got his foot on the marine property ladder he worked his way up from dinghy to rowing boat to motorboat to one-man yacht and now canal boat. He says "If you know what I mean" in a thick accent at the end of every single sentence, I just say "yes" now, partly to hurry the conversation along and partly to avoid finding out if when he says shining shoes and cleaning windows he really means shining shoes and cleaning windows.

Hans has promised he will visit Shropshire as soon as he buys a home that will travel that far.

WEEK 16 DAY 4

Spent the day on the barge watching the world go by. Hans wanted to go "visit my sick Uncle, if you know what I mean", and asked me to look after his barge. I need a day off from saving the world every now and then so I agreed.

WEEK 16 DAY 5

I didn't sleep very well last night, the bed is constantly moving up and down with the ebb and flow of the water. There was a terrible scratching at around midnight and when I went on deck to investigate, there were about a dozen rats running around the barge.

One of them, presumably the leader, was a giant albino thing with teeth like knitting needles and eyes like Morris Minor brake lights. Generally I wouldn't touch a thing like that with a bargepole, but I hit it with a bargepole and it went flying into the water.

I locked myself below deck and waited for sunrise and for the scratching to stop. No sign of Hans. I tried to do what Hans does and sell stuff to tourists.

I'm not terribly good at it. I found some old Nike trainers and offered them as "Clive of India's carpet slippers". No one seemed very interested.

WEEK 16 DAY 6

The people of Amsterdam definitely need help; in the past few days I've hardly met anyone who knows about Shropshire.

Imagine being surrounded by all these museums and all this history but not knowing about the place where all art and culture originated.

I try and speak to as many people as I can, but my Shropshire accent does not seem to command the same interest over here as it did in America and Australia.

I did try to tell a group of Dutch students how all great European art is clearly influenced by the landscape and vibe of Shropshire. It took me half an hour to explain 'vibe' to them. It's a hard word to explain.

Hans came back around teatime, his uncle is much better now apparently. For some reason Hans is now wearing a three-piece suit and a bowler hat, he told me "It is always a good idea to make a first impression that is good to last if you know what I mean."

I'll be very glad when I travel somewhere where everyone speaks English as a first language.

He asked me if I had seen his pet "Pinky", I told him I didn't know what he meant, thanked him and bid him goodbye.

WEEK 16 DAY 7

I'm staying in a hotel now; it's very pleasant with a king-size bed, a Jacuzzi, multi-channel television, tea and coffee making facilities, complimentary biscuits and a lovely view over the rooftops of Amsterdam. I tried to get Channel Four on the television this afternoon to see if Countdown was on but instead I kept stumbling across all sorts of programmes that had nothing to do with conundrums or number puzzles and had far too much nudity. I think I saw a glimpse of Carol Vorderman though.

The streets of Amsterdam are so full of tourists. Most of them have loud shirts, shorts and cameras around their necks. I followed a gaggle of them to see what they do and it seemed to mostly consist of having their photograph taken in front of different buildings.

I left the group at the Van Gogh museum.

Amsterdam is full of museums but I was drawn to the Van Gogh museum as I am quite familiar with his work, in 1997 my Mother had a Van Gogh calendar and we used to have a tea towel with some Van Gogh sunflowers on it until I used it to put out a chip pan fire.

They are having an exhibition called The Musée imaginaire of Van Gogh - "celebrating Vincent van Gogh's 150th birthday". I had no idea he was still alive, I imagine he must be too frail to paint now, they didn't have any of his recent work on display. I'm not sure if he still lives in Amsterdam, if he does it might explain all that ear mutilation business, he was trying to block out the dance music.

There was an old lady in Moreton Say called Edith Romford who used to claim she was well over 100 years old, no-one believed her until she brought a 'congratulations on your 100th birthday' telegram from the Queen dated 1968 to a village meeting. She had to fake her own death in 1989 to avoid all the "oldest woman in Britain" publicity. When I left Moreton Say she was still alive and could often be seen in Market Drayton hitting the "horseless carriages" with her walking stick and complaining about decimalisation.

In the museum they had a reading room with a bank of Internet ready PCs, so I changed the homepage on all of them to my blog index on BBC Shropshire, and the screensavers to a scrolling message "Do you like Van Gogh? Then visit Moreton

Say, it's like one big oil painting". You never know, someone might read that and it could change his or her life.

I bought a new tea towel for Mother at the gift shop; they didn't have any sunflower ones so I got one with a picture of people eating potatoes on it. I'll post it to Moreton Say tomorrow.

WEEK 17 DAY 1

Mother called me, she seems obsessed with the garden.

I always used to mow the lawn, trim the hedge and keep the flowerbeds tidy, and now I have left home to face the myriad threats of the international jet set, she feels I have abandoned my horticultural responsibilities to her. I was under the impression that Toby helped do the garden but Mother made a real issue of it all. I was on the phone for the best part of an hour fielding recriminations and emotional blackmail, but her argument basically boiled down to "you have to come home now, the grass needs cutting".

Needless to say, I once again stressed that my one man mission to bring peace and harmony to the world via the medium of telling people about Shropshire takes precedent over any horticultural responsibilities I may have, and no matter how high the grass grows, or how overrun the path is with dandelions, I shall not be flying home from Amsterdam just to pull up some weeds. I shall not return to my beloved Morton Say until my work is complete and every single man and women realises that the only way to universal harmony is to expand the boundaries of Shropshire until they cover the globe.

I suspect the whole garden thing was not the actual problem and the real issue upsetting her was something else entirely.

WEEK 17 DAY 2

I've been walking around Amsterdam; there really is so much to see here, and so much diversity. I thought the Market Drayton village hall tabletop sale had variety, but Amsterdam almost makes that look like some small-town operation. I actually went in a shop that sells nothing but rubber clothing, with all sorts of bobbly bits, straps and buckles to go with it. Some of the garments seem anatomically suspect and not the sort of thing you would wear in the main street of Market Drayton.

The shop owner, Helga, who bore a quite uncanny resemblance to a woman I used to work with called Theresa who bought me Jammie Dodgers every Thursday, was very receptive to my tales of Shropshire village life. She seemed particularly interested when I told her that nearly everyone in Moreton Say wears rubber, but did not hide her disappointment when I revealed the rubberware was primarily Wellington boots. Despite this, Helga agreed to meet me tonight and show me some of the Amsterdam nightlife.

I'm in my hotel room waiting getting ready, I have to travel light and my choice of clothes is limited. I hope a pair of jeans and an "I've been to Ironbridge" T-shirt are acceptable for a night on the town with Helga. I'm very excited, I haven't been out clubbing since the Moreton Say CE Primary School under-11 disco in 1980.

Helga asked me not to take my palmtop with me ("Morris no play with dinky computer, tonight you play with Helga yes?") so I'll report on my night out when I get back.

WEEK 17 DAY 3

Goodness me.

Last night was a taste of a whole other world. Helga took me to the sort of clubs where the noble sport of Bingo has almost certainly never been played. I had no idea so many people went out at night.

She took me to somewhere called "Escape" first, which was appropriate since all I wanted to do was escape the moment I got there. All I really remember were lots of very sweaty people, constant dance music at ear-splitting levels from speakers the size of bungalows and these inflated white spheres hanging from the ceiling that reminded me of the Rovers from the Prisoner. It was impossible in this atmosphere to tell people about Shropshire so I convinced Helga to show me somewhere else.

This proved to be a mistake. What I meant when I said, "show me somewhere else" was somewhere quieter, possibly somewhere with bingo. I think she misconstrued "show me somewhere else" as a request to see the less savoury aspects of Amsterdam and so Helga took me on a nightmare trip the to the sordid underbelly of the city. A twilight world of private parties, deviants, ambiguous genders, tight clothing and rubber balaclavas, it was all a bit like Telford Town Park on a Thursday night.

Helga translated for me and protected me from any permanent damage; suffice to say I won't be buying instant custard again in a hurry. The night out has made me realise that there are sub-cultures out there so far removed from quiet Shropshire village life that my simple message of harmony and mutual respect may never make any sense to them.

At one party I did meet one really interesting man called Django. I'm not sure what he looked like as his face (and indeed his entire body) was covered with post-it notes. On each of the hundreds of notes different things were written, I couldn't read them as they were in Dutch but I did contribute and wrote "Visit Moreton Say" on one and stuck it on his elbow.

It looked to me like he had used the yellow 38 x 51mm adhesive notes and I was able to give him the order details for the larger size 75 x 75mm ones (Made in Slovenia Order No, 180891) which, if he insisted on covering himself with post-it notes, would provide better coverage and be more cost effective. Django was disproportionately grateful for this advice. He kept saying "Dank je wel" again and again and followed me around for a couple of hours until Helga explained I had to give him a command before he would go away. I asked Helga to tell Django "Put some clothes on and go and live in Shropshire.", Django wrote this on a post-it note, stuck it to his leg and wandered off. He seemed very happy at my instruction, I hope he follows it.

Helga dropped me off at the hotel at about Eight this morning and left "To see her sick Uncle".

I'm resting in my hotel room for the rest of today and mulling over the events of last night.

WEEK 17 DAY 4

The news is talking about SARS and how worried people are about it spreading. I rang home and confirmed there have been no cases in Shropshire yet. Apparently Aunt Felicity had a nasty cough last Tuesday but the doctor said it was more likely to be the 100-a-day cigar habit she has causing it than any oriental virus.

Helga popped in to see me at the hotel, I asked her to translate a paragraph into Dutch for me so I can overcome the language barrier more easily. I'm going to have some leaflets made. The paragraph was –

"Hello. My name is Morris Telford and I come from a small village in Shropshire called Moreton Say. I am travelling the world telling people they would be much better off if they lived in Shropshire. I am in Holland at the moment so if you see me (Photo below) stop me and ask me about how I can help you reach new levels of fulfilment, pleasure and joy without resorting to misusing post-it notes, rubber or instant custard."

I took the text to a printshop along with my passport photo and they are getting several thousand made up for me. I'm also including the URL for the BBC Shropshire website so anyone who gets the leaflet but doesn't catch up with me personally can read my weblog and learn about Shropshire. The leaflets will be ready tomorrow.

I had tea with Helga, she is very open to my ideas about transforming Amsterdam into a larger version of Moreton Say. Every time she gets the opportunity, Helga has vowed to tell people about me and about Moreton Say. We went back to her shop and she put a little sign on the wall, just under the knee clamps, that proclaimed the shop to be officially part of the county of Shropshire. She also promised that in the unlikely event Camilla Edwards ever shops there she will sell her sub-standard latex.

WEEK 17 DAY 5

I've hired a helicopter and I'm gong to do a leaflet drop over the city. The pilot, Javen, is an ex-army helicopter pilot and does tourist flights all over Amsterdam; he boasted to me that he could land a helicopter on a "geldstuk". I don't know what a geldstuk is, or why landing a helicopter on one is something impressive, but I nodded and smiled and told Javen how I wished I could land a helicopter on a geldstuk and it seemed to make him happy.

I have five thousand leaflets in three big bags and I'm sat in the helicopter now looking down on Amsterdam. The people down below look strange from way up here, their heads are like hundreds of little coloured cotton buds jostling between the buildings.
I'm dropping the leaflets now, Javen the helicopter pilot is shouting something at me, but I can't hear him.

We've landed. From what I can gather it is illegal to do a leaflet drop on Amsterdam and the pilot I hired is quite angry. It's strange when someone is angry at you in a foreign language, even though I only understand the odd word, it's really easy to understand his meaning from the tone of his voice and his hand gestures. I think Javen is calling the police so I'm gong to go now.

I'm back at the hotel; it has occurred to me that I should have checked on local law before dropping the leaflets. I suppose from a certain perspective my kind gesture of assistance to the people of Amsterdam could be seem as littering on a grand scale. This is all made worse by the fact that the police now have five thousand pictures of me, I think it might be time to leave.

WEEK 17 DAY 6

I feel the fascinating land of tulips, clogs and elm disease deserves a more thorough examination, it's clear to me that some of these people are in dire need of a little Shropshire in their lives so though Amsterdam is behind me, I'm striking out to see what else Holland has to offer. I'm going to try hitchhiking.

I've fashioned a cardboard sign with the words "hier of daar, ergens" on it. Helga told me this is the thing to write if I want to get picked up quickly. I hope it isn't rude.

I miss Helga, she would have fitted right in at Moreton Say. She would have needed to diversify her stock to make a living there though. Less bondage, more waterproof coats and walking boots.

WEEK 17 DAY 7

I saw my first real windmill today. Tulips surrounded it. I walked up to it from the road and when I knocked on the door a little boy opened it wearing clogs and greeted me warmly.

The whole atmosphere was tarnished when I found out that this was something called a Corporate Theme Windmill. It's where Dutch businessmen go for team building events; the little boy was infact a 37-year-old midget business guru and motivational speaker.

The whole windmill was made of a melded polymer and contained an underground complex of conference rooms, canteens and cheap carpet. The tiny guru soon lost interest in me when he realised I wasn't one of the delegates for the Milk Products Conference and I had to leave.

Windmills should be for milling things, or showing people how things used to be milled, not for some materialistic conglomerate to warp to their own ends. I hate it when people take something old and special and try to mould it to their own needs. IGMT are trying to turn Ironbridge into a multimedia experience, all computers and projectors and interactive facilities.

The money would be much better spent keeping Ironbridge looking like it used to, a magnificent monument to the engineering, architectural and building prowess of times past. Surrounded by majestic countryside and a gateway to a period when innovation and craftsmanship were uneasy partners on a new frontier of bridge construction. I sent IGMT an Email to warn them about the Corporate Theme

Windmill scenario, it will probably just confuse them but at least they will be reading that and not putting a multi-story car park next to Ironbridge.

I've met up with a fellow hitchhiker called Barclay. Barclay looks like a young James K. Polk, he tells me that the only way to see Holland is by Motorcycle, so I'm going to buy him one as soon as we find a shop that sells them. Barclay promises me I will not regret it.

He doesn't know me very well, I don't regret anything.

I don't regret leaving Moreton Say. I don't regret giving up my career in paperclips. I don't regret that I never know what the next day might bring. My life is now one long carnival of wide-eyed wonder and I can't wait to see what tomorrow has in store for me. Wherever the wind of fate blows me, I know there is a small rubber shop in Amsterdam that will be forever Shropshire.

WEEK 18 DAY 1

I'm walking cross-country with my new travelling companion, Barclay. We are looking for a place to buy a motorcycle because Barclay insists it will change my life. I've explained to him that I don't want my life changing, I want to change other people's lives but it fell on deaf ears.

Barclay is a little hard to talk to; he seems bitter or disappointed most of the time, with the occasional period of heavy sighing and eye rolling. I've tried to cheer him up with amusing stories of village life in Shropshire but to no avail.

Even the story about the time my Aunt Felicity accidentally set fire to the tea cosy failed to raise a smile from him.

I miss the casual banter of my fellow Shropshire folk. No one I meet lately wants to talk about bingo or farming or scones.

WEEK 18 DAY 2

The sun is shining on the tulip fields this morning as Barclay and I look for somewhere that sells motorcycles. We are stopping at a small village, no idea what it's called, to have some breakfast.

I asked for a glass of water and some toast at the café where we stopped for breakfast, Barclay had a full Dutch breakfast, which is much like a full English breakfast except with more sausage variations. It's handy having Barclay to help me order food in Holland. Single Dutch is double Dutch to me.

I paid for Barclay who tells me he is 'between jobs'. Apparently he is a qualified air traffic controller. He doesn't get much air traffic control work as he suffers from narcolepsy, which struck me as odd because he also told me he has had narcolepsy since he was quite young. So I asked him why he trained to be an air traffic controller in the first place if he had narcolepsy?

Barclay got terribly defensive at this point. He said he didn't see why his disability should stand in the way of his dream to be an ATC. I told him that that seemed to be the problem, he was dreaming about being an air traffic controller instead of actually controlling air traffic.

He didn't speak to me much after that, he still managed to force down the breakfast I had bought him though.

I must get to know people better before I promise to buy them expensive motorcycles.

Anyway he obviously finds it hard to hold down a job in his chosen profession, when he drops off and a few planes crash I imagine it reflects badly on him. He's sitting opposite me now, not speaking to me. It gives me some time to type my journal though.

I expected the water in the café to be bottled spring water, but all I got was a glass of tap water and it tasted like it had been strained through some old infected bandages. It made me think of the tap water in Moreton Say.

Moreton Say tap water is like the very nectar of the gods, clear, clean, fresh, like a little celebratory march of triumph across your tongue. I'm not sure if they add fluoride or chlorine to it, but at some point in the process it has a little something special added to it. Mother bought a Brita water filter once, it actually made the water taste worse, and it filtered out that Moreton Say tingle. Aunt Felicity told me it was something to do with toxic waste seeping into the ground near our reservoir, but I didn't believe her, I suspect it's some of that old Shropshire magic working it's way into the plumbing.

Barclay apologised to me this afternoon, I think it has something to do with the motorcycle shop we stumbled upon.

WEEK 18 DAY 3

Barclay's mood has improved dramatically.

Yesterday we bought a motorcycle. I say 'we bought', Barclay chose it, and I paid for it. I had promised him I would and now I see the childlike glee on his face, I'm glad I did. I am a bit concerned that this emotional high is not addressing his deeper issues and he really does need to get himself to Shropshire really soon, at least now he has the means of getting there quicker.

We spent the best part of today going very fast around the Dutch countryside, round knee scrapeingly sharp bends and down eye poppingly steep slopes. Conversation was limited to Barclay screaming what sounded like "spoedig cowboy duivel", which I think means something like "speedy cowboy demon", but I could be wrong.

When we stopped briefly to refuel, I asked him where exactly we were going and he said, in what I think was a mock American accent "To Holland back baby!!". I'm quite confused by it all.

I've also noticed Barclay has developed a nervous tick since I bought the bike, his left eyelid flutters and his head leans to one side, it gets worse the more excited he gets. If I didn't believe so firmly in the greater Salopian purpose of my life I might be afraid of him, but I am secure in the knowledge that my mission to tell the world about Shropshire is not yet over and therefore I cannot die.

It has occurred to me that a narcoleptic, manic-depressive with a nervous tick and a man who believes he cannot die are not necessarily a very good road safety combination.

WEEK 18 DAY 4

I asked Barclay again where we are going and I think I got the meaning this time, he said, "To Hell and back, baby!!". He spent last night painting a liquid paper skull onto my rucksack. I wasn't very happy about him doing this, not only has he permanently defaced my bag, but it's a terrible waste and incorrect application of high-grade correction fluid.

I feel like I've been abducted by the twitchy one-man Dutch branch of the Hell's Angels.

Although on the bright side, we did cover a lot of ground today, Barclay only fell asleep twice and both times I was able to wake him up before we hit a bend in the road.

Barclay did offer to stop at a motel but I could hear dance music coming from inside so we rode all night instead.

WEEK 18 DAY 5

The past few days have been a blur. Literally, a blur, I've had an average speed of about 120mph for the last three days.

I fell off the back of the motorbike about an hour ago now. I'm not sure if Barclay noticed I had fallen off, or if he deliberately pushed me off, or if he was asleep and oblivious to everything, but either way he hasn't come back for me yet.

I'm dusty, bruised and stranded by a bleak looking road with nothing but my palmtop and a bag with a crude skull liquid papered onto it for company.

I've had better days.

I scrutinised my map of Holland and I can't quite work out where I am, so nothing to do but keep walking until I see a sign of civilisation.

That's another of the good things about Shropshire, you are never more than a few miles away from a pub, a newsagent or a farm. In Holland the landscape just stretches out flat for miles on end, without even a Little Chef to break the monotony. I'm going to stop following the road and try walking across country more to see what I come across.

WEEK 18 DAY 6

I miss home. I miss watching Ground Force and Countdown. I miss playing Scrabble. Some days my epic journey of world improvement seems like a battle against insurmountable odds. It's like General Custer's last stand, only with less American Indians and more windmills.

When I was younger I used to watch "Champion The Wonder Horse", an old black and white TV series about a wonderful horse called Champion. I think there was a dog in it too. I remember watching the horse gallop across the screen, saving people, righting wrongs. I remember how disappointed I was when I found out it was all filmed in America and not in Shropshire. I once wrote to the BBC suggesting they do a UK version of the series set in Shropshire based on the horse that lived in the field next to our house. It was going to be called "Jonathan the Shropshire Horse", the BBC never replied. It even had the right number of syllables in the title to fit in with the theme tune of the American version.

Perhaps my mistake was writing to the BBC in London, perhaps BBC Shropshire would be interested, I think I still have some of my scripts at home in Moreton Say.

I feel a bit like Jonathan the Shropshire Horse today. Full of potential, desperate to do something, save an attractive young lady that has fallen down a well or drive a busload of underprivileged children to Ironbridge for the day, but no opportunity arises to do good so you end up standing in a field all day instead.

WEEK 18 DAY 7

Feel much better today.

After walking for days I finally found some people. They call themselves the "Rainbow Peace Community" and apparently they set up in the mid-sixties as a social experiment and survived all these years on a winning mixture of friendly, cooperative living, long hair and a thriving worldwide demand for tie-dyed garments.

They all seem to have names that begin with a colour and end with a creature, the leader of the community is called Gold Dove, his second is called Amber Puma, their children are called Saffron Weasel, Aquafortis Goat, Vermillion Seahorse, Copper Mantis and Brown Cow.

I think Brown Cow got the short straw there.

I get to choose my honorary name during my stay here. I have chosen Cyan Badger; it has a Shropshire ring to it. I think.

They are a third generation community now and some of them have never left the small insular society they were born into. I find this sort of inhibitive upbringing very worrying, how will they ever come to know the glory of Shropshire unless they are exposed to the outside world? It's all very well staying put if you are fortunate enough to be born in Shropshire, but there really is no excuse at all for parent's outside the West Midlands not allowing their children the opportunity to discover Shropshire for themselves. It's just cruel.

They have invited me to stay and I have accepted, for the moment. In a few days I hope they will absorb my tales of Shropshire life, cut their hair and become another outpost for the Cyan Badger way of living. We shall see.

WEEK 19 DAY 1

The "Peace Feast" last night had more in common with a Moreton Say parish summer barbecue than I expected. It was basically lots of very nice people with slightly odd names eating burnt sausages and wearing tie-dye garments. I gave a little speech at the feast, told them all how I am on a one-man mission to change the world into one big Shropshire, how I live by my wits and forge my own path through the dark night of uncertainty that has cloaked the world. I threw in a bit about some of my recent life-changing successes and bizarre travels and described myself as Shropshire's answer to Jack Kerouac.

They seemed suitably impressed.

Some of them even knew who Jack Kerouac was.

I'm currently living with the "Rainbow Peace Community" somewhere in Holland. They own a segregated compound of prefabricated but environmentally friendly homes and live a lifestyle of love, sharing, honesty and long-hair. I have adopted the commune title Cyan Badger for my stay here and already I feel I am having a positive effect on them.

Today I was guest speaker at their little school. I told all the children about how wonderful a place Shropshire is, how everyone there is nice and kind to each other all of the time, how the land sings with unspoilt beauty and how they must leave the commune and move there as soon as they are older. I spiced things up a bit by telling them that if they didn't leave the commune by the time they were 18 the diseased rat monsters from the forest of death would come and take them away to work as slaves in the saliva mines. I think that did the trick with some of the children, unfortunately the teacher came back in and I finished with a story about Jonathan the Shropshire Horse.

WEEK 19 DAY 2

The commune leader, Gold Dove, came and had a word with me about my classroom talk yesterday. I was honest with him and told him I just encouraged the children to widen their horizons a bit with a colourful tale. He actually seemed quite receptive to my ideas that Shropshire could represent a new stage in the evolution of the "Rainbow Peace Community" and we talked for the best part of the day.

They eat a lot of seeds here. They have big bags of them all over and everyone seems to spend a lot of time eating them. I can't see the attraction myself. I always thought the seeds were the bit you throw away. I tried making a sandwich out of them but sesame seeds and poppy seeds just aren't the same as jam.

I've been accepted into their little community here very quickly, and a lot of the younger people come to me for advice. Essentially the answer to most of their problems is "move to Shropshire" but I try to word it differently to suit each case. They have painted a large blue badger mural on the side of the prefab I am sleeping in as a sign that I am one of them; I'm quite flattered by their gesture, though unimpressed by their depiction of the noble badger.

They seem to burn a lot of incense here. Every home has some bizarre coloured cloud hovering around it. I asked Ruby Yak about this, she said it helped them calm their thoughts and be at one with their surroundings. I think it's to mask the smell of the chemical toilets.

I've arranged for a travel company to take a coach load of people from the community here to see Shropshire. All expenses paid one-way trip to the land of goodness. I haven't told Gold Dove yet; I want it to be a surprise.

WEEK 19 DAY 3

Today I was given the great honour of naming a new child, a little girl that had been born the day before. Each new member is given a commune name, a creature and a colour. The creature represents the commune's commitment to the earth and the environment, symbolically bonding each member with nature and the ecosystem. The colour represents their love of art, diversity and beauty. Gold Dove, Turquoise Antelope (the mother) and Purple Stallion (the father) all suggested names to try and help me decide but they insisted the final choice was mine as an honoured guest.

None of them looked terribly happy as I held little Red Herring and told them how lovely she was. She looks a bit like a very, very young Vivien Leigh, only bald and dribbling.

I also tried to talk to an assembled group about the importance of diversification. I told them that it's all very well living in a self-contained society, but if you don't leave every now and then you'll never find out how much better off you are staying put. That's certainly something I have learned. I took some names for a provisional list of people that want to book a seat on the coach to Shropshire next week.

Gold Dove came to see me this evening about my planned coach trip. He wasn't very pleased. It seems he had rather hoped that I would be the one to stay with them. I had to tell him frankly that he would never be able to compete with Moreton Say. Moreton Say is such a tight-knit society it makes the "Rainbow Peace Community" look like a bunch of hippies with silly names sat in caravans avoiding reality.

I could have put it a bit more tactfully, but he got the idea

WEEK 19 DAY 4

The coach trip is off.

Each of the names I gathered has approached me individually and asked to be removed from my planned outing. Gold Dove is obviously motivating them to do this, I can see him constantly in the background with his arms folded and his face grim. I smiled my best Moreton Say smile back at him and it had no effect.

I don't feel so welcome here anymore, Pink Mongoose isn't speaking to me and someone has written "Cyan Badger est atati rangui" underneath my mural. I don't know what "Cyan Badger est atati rangui" means but I'm pretty sure it's not praising me for how well I can organise coach trips at short notice.

All this "Peace and Love" stuff is actually wearing a bit thin already, I get the feeling there is an undercurrent of repression in this apparently blissful society. I tried to have a quiet chat with some of the younger people who had previously signed up for my coach outing, not even Olive Marmoset would talk to me about why they no longer wanted to visit Shropshire.

Also, last night when they thought I was asleep, a tape was switched on just outside the open window of my prefabricated temporary home. It sounded like sitar music and a low droning voice saying "You love it here, you will stay. You love it here, you will stay", over and over and over again. I had to put some headphones on and listen to a tape I had of Radio Shropshire just to get to sleep.

WEEK 19 DAY 5

It was a lovely day today, if I closed my eyes I could almost imagine I was back in Moreton Say, bathing in the soothing rays of the Shropshire sun and listening to Aunt Felicity talk about her time as a debt collector in Glasgow.

For a while I tried to drum up a bit of enthusiasm among the commune for a game of Bingo, but no one was very keen. I even collected a load of eggs and wrote the number 1 to 49 on them, but they proved to be inadequate substitutes for bingo balls, especially when I put them all in a barrel and spun it around. Gold Dove was looking forward to an omelette for breakfast, so that didn't help me ingratiate myself to him much either.

I sneaked out this evening and had a look around camp to see if I could find any clues. You'll never guess what I saw. A copy of "Country Life" on a table in Gold Dove's home. Aha. Why would someone who professes to want nothing to do with the outside world be reading about English Country Life? I bet Gold Dove comes from Devon. That would explain a lot.

I found the tape they put outside my window last night with the "You love it here, you will stay" message. I re-recorded it to say, "You can leave here, for Moreton Say" and left it outside Gold Dove's window. You never know.

WEEK 19 DAY 6

It all turned a bit sour today. If I didn't know they were all committed vegetarians I might be afraid they were going to eat me.

Gold Dove confronted me with the tape and asked me what I thought I was doing. I told him I was hoping to use his own brainwashing methods to deprogram him so he could see the true face of this warped little commune, lead a mass exodus from the Rainbow Peace Community and come to appreciate the real life in Shropshire instead.

It wasn't the answer he was looking for.

I've been asked to leave.

I feel a bit like Henry Bathman.

Henry Bathman came to live in Moreton Say in 1992. He bought the cottage by the cesspit and wanted to turn it into rented holiday accommodation. Of course the parish council voted against turning the village into some sort of glorified Butlins and forbade him to do so. When he refused to listen to their authority and started to fit things like double glazing and an inside toilet to the cottage, he was, of course, stripped naked, tarred and feathered and driven out by the customary screaming horde of angry villagers.

I feel a bit like Henry being asked to leave like this, only in my case it's totally unfair.

I'd be hard pressed to say that my time with the commune had been a resounding success for Shropshire/Holland relations, but at least I've planted that seed of doubt in some of the younger minds of the community.

That coach is still booked for next week too, maybe when it turns up a few might make a dash for it. I've done all I can. Back to the life of a lonesome traveller.

WEEK 19 DAY 7

Mother called me to tell me that the man came to read the electricity meter today. I asked her how Toby and Sophia are getting along; she told me that the man read their meter too.

I was grateful she called but struggled to see the relevance of her information. Perhaps it's a code.

I've received this message on the BBC Message Board from Bridget Fixitt -

"Morris, a town needs your help! Please visit Gorinchem in Holland (just north of Breda) The word about you is spreading, and you may have made some web disciples there. The people there uncannily resemble Shropshire folk, but are trapped in their Dutch ways. Ban the bike! Up with Morris!"

Never one to dwell on failure, I'm on the road again now, trying to work out where Gorinchem is. I don't have a map with me now so I'm just going past the second windmill to the right and straight on till morning.

WEEK 20 DAY 1

I'm in Holland, I'm not quite sure where in Holland. It all looks the same to me. The terrain here is as flat as a fresh pack of A4 copier paper and considerably less interesting.

I'm not feeling like myself today, the last week was a bit of a disappointment. I had great plans for persuading a commune to move en masse to Shropshire. They didn't. They kicked me out.

I hate getting kicked out of places. I never got kicked out of anywhere in Moreton Say. Mr Derby didn't get kicked out of the village's weekly Bingo game when he developed Yemeks syndrome, even Mrs Ingot didn't get kicked out of Market Drayton village hall when she was caught selling out-of–date scones. I got kicked out of that commune just for trying to arrange a nice coach trip to Shropshire. It's all so wrong.

Yemeks syndrome is a sort of milder, bingo related version of Tourettes syndrome. You don't shout out obscenities, but instead shout out random numbers and occasionally "HOUSE". It played havoc with the weekly bingo for years.

Fortunately Mr Derby had his tongue ripped out in a freak fan-belt accident in 1998 and after that he no longer disturbed the game so much.

I'm trying to hitchhike my way to Gorinchem, which apparently is just north of Breda; I'm not having a great deal of success. Five people have stopped so far, they all followed the same pattern, they ask me something in Dutch, I respond loudly and slowly that I do not understand and they then drive off. I need a new strategy if I'm going to get anywhere.

The Dutch language is to my mind very like the European Monetary Union, I just don't understand it.

I'm going to go somewhere where they speak English next; it's very frustrating having all this knowledge and information about Shropshire and not being able to make people understand you. Also, I always have this sneaking suspicion that people in Holland do understand me, they just pretend not to. Like when that last car stopped and I said, "I don't speak Dutch, I come from Shropshire, can I have a lift please?" the driver's mouth was saying something Dutch and apologetic sounding but his eyes were full of hate and fear.

I read somewhere (It might have been the Moreton Say Parish magazine "The Purity, Bingo and Bee-keeping Gazetteer") that by 2023 everyone outside Shropshire would be so paranoid about burglary, mugging, fraud, murder, kidnapping and escaped convicts that no-one would talk to anyone else at all. It just occurred to me, that this only gives me 20 more years to get everyone to move to Shropshire, I've got a lot of ground to cover.

WEEK 20 DAY 2

I met a lady today called Elaine who bore a quite stunning resemblance to Oliver Hardy, only without the moustache and the back catalogue of silent movies.

Elaine lives in a one-room house out in the Dutch countryside with her seventeen cats and some quite breathtaking odours. I had dinner with Elaine, who despite obvious hygiene issues seems very content and she promised to visit Shropshire first chance she gets.

The really interesting thing about Elaine was her ability to communicate with her feline companions. I offered to cat-sit while she makes the trip, but she declined.

WEEK 20, DAY 3

My Mother always used to say you can tell a lot about a person from their shoes and their haircut. Not only is this excellent advice for life, but it also explains why she never liked the barefoot bald man that lived in that disused milk depot outside Oswestry.

So today I bought a new pair of boots, very smart, very shiny, purposeful boots, the sort of boots you might conquer the Wrekin with. I also had a haircut.

I tried to chat to the barber but he just kept agreeing with me every time I asked him a question. It was very irritating.

"How long have you lived here?"

"Yes"

"If you moved is there anywhere in particular you would like to move to?"

"Yes, yes"

"How much is a haircut here?"

"Mmmm, Yes."

"Do you speak English?"

"Yes"

"You don't do you?"

"Yes, sir"

You get the idea. It wasn't a bad haircut though. Apparently I'm not all that far from Gorinchem, I'm on a bus there right now.

WEEK 20 DAY 4

I've arrived in the town of Gorinchem. I've been told the people here uncannily resemble Shropshire folk, but are trapped in their Dutch ways. I'm staying in a little hotel and getting the feel of the place. I can sense it is ripe. The very streets of Gorinchem will soon cry out with a long buried yearning for all things Shropshire, mark my words.

There's not really much here in Gorinchem to make people want to stay, I feel sure that once I get chance to speak to them they will understand how much better off they will be in Shropshire. I've found someone who is prepared to translate a speech for me and I'm planning to speak to the people tomorrow.

In the meantime I've been trying to meet people on a one to one basis, but it's really difficult, less people seem to speak English here than they did in Amsterdam.

I found a lovely little shop and bought a "Learn Dutch" book and tape, but none of the phrases in it helped me much. I don't need "Where is the toilet", or "Two sandwiches please", or "The weather is fine today", I want "Come and live in Shropshire", "Have you any idea how lovely Market Drayton is at this time of year?" or "If only you would learn about the idyllic life that can be yours for the taking in Shropshire I'm sure you would agree to go there, here take this plane ticket and let me be the alarm call that wakes you from this Dutch nightmare and helps you embark on a wonderful journey into the real life in Shropshire."

WEEK 20 DAY 5

I gave a speech in the town square today, I generally make these things up as I go along, but I had to have this translated so I could give it phonetically. I thought I'd share the transcript with you-

"Good Afternoon good people. Thank you for coming. My name is Morris Telford, I come to you from the Shropshire village of Moreton Say and I am here to change your life for the better.

There are essentially three types of people in this world. People who are born in Shropshire, people who move to Shropshire and, sadly the largest group, people who never see Shropshire.

Don't worry. I'm here to balance the scales.

I've been travelling all over the world as an emissary for the sacred pleasures of Shropshire life, a herald of the unspoken beauty that fills England's finest county, a solid platinum bell ringing in a new era of Salopian understanding and peace, a lightning flash of sudden revelations in the dark night of ignorance, an ethereal guiding hand to push you towards Shropshire and all it holds for you, a signpost of reason at the crossroads of confusion, an explosion of common sense in a firework factory of misguided acts. I am your magical master butcher in the meat market of inferior, diseased animal parts, your buy one get one free special offer of a lifetime in the freezer aisle of the global supermarket, your heavy duty stapler of truth in the stationary cupboard of deceit, your giant squid of retribution in the stormy sea of guilt, your only Cuban cigar in the last chance box of smoking opportunity, your own personal representative in the tumultuous, disorientating whirlwind of package lifestyles and your last, best hope for escaping the hideous life you now lead and embarking on a superlative voyage of destiny to the very heart of the golden county, Shropshire."

I think it must have lost something in translation. The crowd just seemed bewildered after I gave my speech and dispersed like as many autumn leaves leaving a leafy pile of leaves.

WEEK 20 DAY 6

I'm leaving Holland.

I'm fed up.

Not one person came up to me after my speech yesterday, and I was a bit nervous giving it too. I can count the times I've been nervous on one hand. There was that time I tried to climb the church at Moreton Say after a school friend told me Clive of India lived on the roof. There was the time I stood up at the annual general meeting of the parish council and complained about the inferior standard of the Bingo markers they use at the weekly game, specifically the low tone ink. Then there was the time I accidentally stapled my hand to the desk during an important meeting with Mr Magson, and lastly I remember was the time I got home late from work on Tuesday 8th January 2002 and nearly met my next-door neighbour Sophia in the flesh. Those and the speech yesterday are about it, and I got all nervous yesterday for nothing, no one responded.

I'm going to Germany; see if I can fight some Nazis or something.

WEEK 20 DAY 7

Coach leaves tonight, as a parting gesture to Gorinchem I've managed to get a mailing list of every person who lives here from the town hall, I'm getting a local mailing company to send them all my mother's phone number on a small postcard, maybe she will be able to talk some sense into some of them. She's always complaining no one rings her.

I sent Mother a lingua-phone "Learn Dutch" tape and book in the post so she can prepare a few helpful phrases for the 104,392 Dutch people who now have her phone number.

I don't know much about Germany, but I notice Melvin Bone suggests I give it a go. Melvin also says-

"Here is a quote from Country Life "Anyone who knows Devon could have guessed it would do well in this contest. Even so, no one could possibly have predicted the county would rub its rivals' faces so deeply in the mud."

Shropshire scored a poor 2 out of 10 for tranquillity, but did better elsewhere scoring 10 out of 10 for burglaries………….. Morris, your mission will succeed if you transfer your allegiance to Devon. I'll endeavour to send you some scrumpy and fudge to get you started."

Either Melvin works for the evil Country Life or has been through some sort of sophisticated brain tampering process to say such terrible things.

I would like to respond to a couple of the more hurtful things Mel said.

Tranquillity was invented in Shropshire. Archaeological evidence that I have seen with my own eyes in the Market Drayton secret museum clearly shows that while the people of Devon were still trying to walk upright and build rudimentary dwellings, the people of Shropshire were developing an eco-friendly, peace loving society, pushing the boundaries of tranquillity by sitting in their gardens with a good book and a nice cup of tea.

Scrumpy and Fudge? Obviously it would take much more than apple juice and inferior confectionary to turn anyone from the Shropshire delights of gingerbread and the 130 percent Moreton Say rum that the vicar distills.

As for burglaries, the last reported burglary in Moreton Say was in 1898 when Terrence Threefold broke into Mrs Constance Rhetoric's barn and tried to make off with a spade, a leather water pouch and a sack of flour. He was caught and hanged before he had chance to dig, drink or make a cake.

Where was Mr Threefold from?

Devon.

WEEK 21 DAY 1

I've had a very exciting day today.

I'm on a coach to Germany, though thankfully a good proportion of my fellow passengers speak English and I have been able to lead a rousing singsong medley of Shropshire based songs.

It took a while to get some of them to learn the words correctly, but the emergency door is broken so they had little choice but to sit and listen. I love a captive audience.

After the singing came my anecdotes of Shropshire village life. I told the one about Mr Gantry's broken chimney pot collection, he only had five but he loved them like children.

I covered the period from 1989 to 1993 when strange lights appeared in the sky every Tuesday night and all the cows around Moreton Say inexplicably stopped eating and whistled gently all night long.

I also gave a lengthy talk on how much better life is in Shropshire that went down very well with those still awake.

I genuinely think that I could have convinced the driver to turn the coach around there and then and drive to Shropshire if it hadn't been for the little sign that said we couldn't talk to him.

The coach driver's name badge says he is called "Ignatius", not a name you hear very often.

WEEK 21 DAY 2

The coach has broken down. Ignatius, who bears a quite uncanny resemblance to Keith Gordon in his Static and Christine days, before his hair fell out and he became a director, is holding a spanner and tutting a lot.

Keith Gordon is a really good director, I love Keith Gordon films, there's Shropshire blood in there somewhere, I'm sure. Not sure if Keith can drive a coach though.

An increasingly large black cloud is coming from the side of the coach. Ignatius calls the coach Lucy, after his maternal grandmother. This is the only communication I've had with Ignatius, when I asked him why he kept stroking the side of the front wheel arch and saying "Lucy, oh Lucy", I asked him why and he told me.

Since then all attempts at communication have been thwarted. Ignatius has the little sign that says "Do not talk to the driver" with him at all times and gets it out every time I try to ask him something.

On one occasion, when I persisted, he pressed the sign into my face. I sense he does not want to bond with me, perhaps he heard snippets of my Shropshire anecdotes and fears if he hears more he will be compelled to change his road warrior lifestyle.

We've been stuck at the side of the road for over three hours now.

My fellow passengers are tiring and getting restless despite my attempts to keep their spirits high with continued tales of the good life in Shropshire. One of the older ladies has covered her ears with her hands and is rocking back and forth in her seat murmuring to herself. I'm sensing she is tired of my stories, you can sometimes have too much of a good thing.

Ignatius has gone.

Without saying a word to us, he walked up the road. Hopefully he has gone for help, or petrol, or a mechanic, or perhaps he has just stranded us all here in the middle on somewhere with nothing but four egg sandwiches, half a Toblerone and an apple to sustain 29 people. Either way, it's not very good customer service.

A large man with ridiculous sideburns has appointed himself leader and is taking a vote on whether we should stay the night. I voted yes, so did 21 others so we are sleeping in the coach. What an excellent opportunity to finish educating these good people about Shropshire and its inhabitants.

WEEK 21 DAY 3

It was cold last night and some of us shared body heat to maintain warmth. I got a little closer than I really wanted to with a 46-year old German pet therapist called Mavis.

I had planned to stay up late telling rousing tales about Moreton Say and its surroundings, but I was stopped before I got started by a militant faction that seems suddenly anti-Shropshire. I think I spotted a Devon accent in there somewhere.

Someone, not sure who, has managed to get the coach running and we are on the road again. I feel a bit like I'm being hijacked. We passed Ignatius walking back down the road and he waved his fists and screamed at us as we flew by, I think he threw his little "Don't talk to the driver" sign at us too. Personally I think we should have stopped and picked him up, but I was outnumbered by the others.

The atmosphere is actually quite tense on board the coach now. I'm think I'm going to cheer everyone up with a few Shropshire based anecdotes. I have a really good feeling about this whole situation.

WEEK 21 DAY 4

HELLO.

MY NAME IS MAVIS.

MORRIS HE HAS ASKED ME TO BE WRITING HIS DIARY FOR HIM.

YESTERDAY MORRIS TRIED TO TELL US HIS STORIES AGAIN.

IT IS THE THIRD TIME WE HAVE HEARD ABOUT MRS GANTRY'S CHIMNEY POT COLLECTION. IT MAKE SOME PEOPLE VERY MAD. THEY TIE MORRIS UP.

I AM A PET THERAPIST. I CAN MAKE ALSATIANS HAPPY. ANIMALS ARE MUCH CLEANER THAN HUMANS. ANIMALS ARE MY FRIENDS. MY ONLY FRIENDS.

WEEK 21 DAY 5

TODAY WE STOP FOR FOOD. HANSEL IS DRIVING NOW. I LIKE HANSEL HE IS A GOOD MAN. HE PROMISES WE MAKE IT TO GERMANY.

I HAVE BEEN COMBING MORRIS HAIR TODAY. I LIKE MORRIS. HE IS KIND MAN. I LIKE HIS CLOTHES TOO. SENSIBLE CLOTHES. LIKE A TEACHER OR A FATHER.

MORRIS SAYS TO TELL YOU DO NOT WORRY. MORRIS SAY HE CHUCKLES IN THE FACE OF ADVERSITY AND HE IS A GIANT GOLDEN DRAGON OF FREEDOM OR SOMETHING LIKE THAT. MORRIS SPEAKS IN A FUNNY WAY. I LIKE IT.

MORRIS SAYS COUNTRY LIFE ARE BEHIND SOMETHING. I DON'T UNDERSTAND HIM.

WHEN MORRIS TALK TO ME I FEEL LIKE A DIFFERENT PERSON. MORRIS IS VERY SPECIAL. MORRIS TALKS TO ME LIKE HE KNOWS ME WELL. MORRIS WOULD MAKE A GOOD HUSBAND.

WEEK 21 DAY 6

SOME OF THE WOMEN ARE CRYING. THEY ARE WEAK LIKE PUPPIES. I AM STRONG LIKE A PEDIGREE HUNTER. ANIMALS ARE MUCH EASIER TO UNDERSTAND THAN HUMANS. ALSATIAN NEVER HIJACK COACHES.

MORRIS IS TRYING TO TELL ME SOMETHING BUT HANSEL HAS TAPED HIS MOUTH. I FEED MORRIS TODAY WITH STRAW THROUGH HOLE IN TAPE. CUP OF SOUP TOO HOT FOR MORRIS. MORRIS BURN HIS CHIN.

MORRIS MOTHER HAS RINGING ME ON MOBILE TELEPHONE. SHE WORRIED ABOUT GRASS CUTTING. I TELL HER EVERYTHING JUST FINE NOT TO WORRY. MORRIS MOTHER START ASKING ME IF I AM MORRIS GIRLFRIEND.

I SAY YES. I LIKE MORRIS.

MORRIS MOTHER BEGIN SHOUTING. I HANG UP.

MORRIS MOTHER RING AGAIN. I TELL HER SHE NEEDS TO BE MORE LIKE CAT. RELAX MORE AND ACCEPT THINGS.

MORRIS MOTHER BEGIN SHOUTING AGAIN. I HANG UP.

WEEK 21 DAY 7

POLICE HELICOPTER IS FOLLOWING US NOW. WE DID NOT PAY FOR FUEL AT LAST STATION AND THIS WAS A MISTAKE. HANSEL IS SHOUTING A LOT. MAYBE HANSEL NOT SUCH A GOOD MAN. HANSEL DRIVING VERY MUCH FAST.

POLICE CARS ARE FOLLOWING COACH NOW. MORRIS WAS TIED UP AND FELL OUT OF HIS SEAT. I THINK HE MIGHT BE DEAD.

I LIKE MORRIS. HE HAS SOFT HAIR LIKE BABY.

WEEK 22 DAY 1

I've had a very troubling few days.

I've been hanging onto life by the slightest of threads.

I've diced with death, discoed across the dance floor of deadly destiny and stayed alive.

I've played my hand and very nearly got a voided card in the great bingo game of life but have nevertheless emerged victorious and with only mild concussion and a little bruising.

I was unfortunate enough to get caught up in a coach hijacking. I've been tied up, knocked unconsciousness and had my hair combed against my will.

The police managed to stop the coach at their third roadblock; they shot out the tyres and Hansel surrendered. At first he tried to pin it all on me, told the police I was a Shropshirian Fundamentalist and wanted to make myself into a martyr for the holy cause. When all the police found in my bag were some bingo markers, post-it notes and unwashed clothes they decided I was no real threat.

Mavis gave me back my palmtop before a tearful farewell, she had grown ferociously attached to me while I was tied up at the back of the coach.

Once again I had to explain to a smitten female that I must walk my path alone, though I must admit that making the sacrifice to remain unattached was a bit easier this time thanks to Mavis, her appearance, the fact that she smelled of wet dog and that she kept touching my hair - I hate that.

The police gave me a lift to the nearest town, a place called Oberwesel that I think is near the River Rhein. After some difficulty making myself understood I've booked into a hotel to gather my thoughts and keep a low profile.

Mother rang and I had to explain about Mavis answering my phone and saying we were romantically involved, I tried to say it was all a simple misunderstanding and a stranger had picked up my phone, I didn't want her to worry.

Mother did not sound convinced so I told her that I had secretly got married to Mavis last week and we were on our honeymoon. Mother didn't believe that either so I told her due to the stress of constant travel I had developed a multiple personality disorder and I spent four hours every day as a female alter-ego with a split-end fixation and a thick German accent.

Mother was having none of it so I gave up and explained that Mavis was a delusional pet therapist that got hold of my phone while I was tied up on a coach that had been hijacked.

Oddly she believed me. Despite her failings, my Mother still possesses that uncanny maternal ability to know when I'm lying. She can also tell when I'm biting my nails, not eating properly, wearing unsavoury underwear or staying up past 11 o'clock, even if I'm on the other side of the world. It worries me.

WEEK 22 DAY 2

My hotel in Oberwesel is, by a fortuitous turn of events, staging a European poetry convention, "The River Of Words" with competitions, readings, book signings and as much German sausage as you can eat. It's multilingual so I have entered myself in the freeform expression category. I see this as an excellent opportunity to not only tell people about Shropshire, but also to display my prowess with the myriad subtleties of the English language, my dextrous wordplay and my uncanny usage of the mixed metaphor.

I'm going to try out a verse I wrote a few years ago called "Moreton Say, I love you", it's about Moreton Say and my love for it there.

Staying at my hotel is another English poet called John Yeovil who looks not unlike Val "Iceman" Kilmer when he was in Top Gun, only less flying jump jets and more rhyming couplets.

John travels the world, much like myself, sharing his thoughts with the people he meets, the main difference between us is that John isn't so bothered about changing the world for the better, he just wants to be rich and famous. This self-centred outlook is probably due to his upbringing, he comes from Devon. He has my pity.

I explained to John the double truth that money does not buy happiness and fame is a cage of fear. He wrote it down. John writes down a lot of what I say, he says it's for inspiration, I think it's so he can pretend he thought of it first.

Tonight I do my first public reading.

WEEK 22 DAY 3

I went down a storm. I've decided to spread my message through the medium of poetry and verse.

MORETON SAY, I LOVE YOU
By MORRIS TELFORD

"Tumbling hills of gentle good
Oswestry, Marchamley Wood
Simple fields of pure and calm
Market Drayton, Old Bill's Farm

Moreton Say I love you so.
Why do I love you? I don't know.
So many things for me to choose.
So lucky to be of the few

That live there.

Will you be my Valentine?
I'll buy you flowers and some cheap wine
I'll always be true and loyal and I'll
think of you with a genuine smile.

In the marvellous chocolate box of life
You are the soft centre, a whippy whirl.
And though perhaps initially disappointing to those who wanted a toffee
Turns out to be the favourite after all.

I've lived in you, I was born in you
I climbed my first tree, you were there too.
I'll never leave until I do,

and even then, I'll bring you too.
Part of Shropshire, part of me
Bingo at dinner, Countdown at tea
Better than ordering stationary
Moreton Say will you be

My one true love?

Moreton Say I love you.
Do you love me too?
I like to think so."

WEEK 22 DAY 4

I'm in the quarter-finals, my competition seems slight. I don't like to blow my own trumpet, but in the next heat I am going on after a woman called Jessica who just grunts, screams and occasionally shouts "my boyfriend has left me" while she holds a balloon between her knees. She calls it – "a primal response to the systematic repression of womankind". I call it a mad woman with a balloon between her legs shouting about her boyfriend leaving her. She doesn't stand a chance against my latest epic that I penned last night – "Bingo Markers Of The World"

BINGO MARKERS OF THE WORLD
By MORRIS TELFORD

"Bingo is a noble thing
With many advantages
Cash prizes you can win
by incremental stages.

One of the best things about Bingo
And it's an aspect that's often ignored
Is the special marker that you use
To cross numbers off your card

Not just any old pen or pencil
Felt-tip or marker will do
It's important to choose a superior quality
Bingo marker to use.

Some Bingo markers are angry
They flake and leak all the time
These are no good for bingo
As they draw an inferior line.

Some Bingo markers are timid
They run out and don't mark anymore
They are just as bad as the angry ones
I mentioned the verse before.

Other Bingo markers are weaklings
And can snap if submitted to strain
I had one like that once in 1992
It completely ruined my game.

Where your marker comes from
Can be important too
The notorious Singapore markers
Were made with inferior glue

I once had one made in China
That only lasted a day
Though to be fair, Oriental markers
Are generally ok.

The finest marker I've ever had
I bought in Market Drayton
From Rosemary the newsagents
Next to the railway station.

I called that marker Elvira
And loved her like a girl
She was stolen from me a few weeks ago
On my mission to save the world.

I miss her tender grip
The way she'd hesitate
Before striking through the numbers
Two fat ladies, eighty-eight

Her colour and her balance
Her simple, even line
The way I felt she looked at me
And said "Morris, you're mine"

I never will forget her
Nestled at my side
My Whitely to her Voderman
Her Bonnie to my Clyde.

I now tend to use the American
Twin nibbed fluorescent pen
They're not as good as Elvira
I'd give them a six out of ten."

WEEK 22 DAY 5

I don't believe it. Jessica beat me in the quarter-final. The judges felt her "primal rage and innovative balloon use outweighed the more traditional verse".

One woman in the audience was moved to tears by my Bingo Markers poem. I'm absolutely stunned. I'm very happy that Jessica will now have the opportunity to hold a balloon between her knees and scream in the semi-finals though; I congratulated her with a firm handshake and not the slightest twinge of bitterness.

Art is a difficult animal to categorise, I always think the important thing is to be happy with your own work, so I'm going to continue to write my epic poem "How many ways do I love Shropshire?" and send it to my Mother when it's finished, she always enjoys my work.

I wrote this today-

WHY I DIDN'T WIN

By MORRIS TELFORD

"Instead of concentrating on the subtleties of language,

where thought and mind harmonise.

I should have just shouted a load of nonsense

with a balloon between my thighs."

Despite my defeat, an American publisher did approach me and express an interest in a book of Shropshire related verse; I'll let you know if it's ever published. A provisional title is "Morris Telford's Shropshire Verse", and will include "Bingo Markers of The World", "Moreton Say I Love You", "Shropshire The Golden Land of Love, Joy and Gingerbread", "Why Can't Everyone Just Be Nice To Each Other Like They Are In Moreton Say?", "Things That Carol Voderman Reminds Me Of" and "Camilla Edwards Lies, Lies, Lies".

WEEK 22 DAY 6

I stayed up late last night, drinking at the bar with the poet John Yeovil. Despite being from Devon, John seems to have a great appreciation of beauty and told me about his world travels.

He told me about the time he went swimming naked in the Amazon, and the time he lived with Eskimos during the four month night of Hari-Kancha.

Since beginning his travels he's played death poker in illegal Mexican gambling pits, sampled the thousand pleasures of Moroccan love dens, base jumped from the Hong Kong finance centre with his hair on fire, seen the hidden underground mirror temples of platinum in South America and the Art dungeons of Paris but is still seeking that ultimate experience, the Holy Grail of life events.

He's searching for the one single crystal clear moment of joy and fulfillment where he knows his travels are at an end and he has seen the true face of creation.

I, of course, told him he must visit Moreton Say, all he wants is waiting for him there.

What a shame we didn't meet years ago, I could have saved him so much trouble.

One thing John did say that intrigued me were his experiences of China, he said the regime there is in some ways very oppressive, but the people are eager for new ideas and there is a strong underground current of change. Bingo is also very popular.

I decided to travel to China, from what John says it sounds right up my street. I don't really know much about China; they seem to make a lot of the colourful plastic toys for the Market Drayton stalls so I imagine they know all about Shropshire.

WEEK 22 DAY 7

Getting a flight to China has proved more difficult than I imagined, the Chinese authorities aren't overly keen on admitting people whose stated reason for travel is "to turn over the current regime and get the populous to move to Shropshire". I changed the reason to "holiday and cultural exchange" and that seemed to do the trick, I fly from Frankfurt airport next week.

I've been checking the BBC message board and notice Melvin Bone has taken the time to write again.

"I am amazed by the response to my last posting. I have been informed by the Devon Tourist Board that visits by Dutch people have trebled since my last posting inviting the Dutch to come and visit. Apparently in Holland they are living in fear of a Northener wandering their country extolling the virtues of the barren north of England. I have heard many have taken up jobs in Devon as they recognise it as a truly glorious place to live."

This is clearly not true. I myself called the Devon Tourist Board, after about five minutes someone picked up the phone and thanked me for calling, it was the first query they have had in seventeen years.

"Morris: I'm sure that Shropshire was indeed once an idyllic place and Devon a backward backwater. But as the Country Life survey highlighted Devon has been able to move on and flourish to achieve greatness as a county, meanwhile Shropshire has unfortunately stagnated. I looked up the last crime you mentioned in Shropshire. You are right in one aspect, the last crime in Shropshire of the 19th century took place in 1898. I fear however you textbook may cover only the 19th Century as crime has escalated throughout he 20th Century and into the 21st. The 'Most Wanted' at the moment is a self styled "Stationary Bandit" who has fled the country. If you meet such a fellow on your travels watch out as Police have him listed as armed with industrial staplers and dangerous."

At first I was very worried about this information and called my Mother to warn her not to open the door to anyone brandishing a stapler. Then I realised you are making some sort of connection to me and this fictional "Stationary Bandit", though of course anyone who knows me will tell you I always adhere to and take very seriously the Health and Safety regulations when using Industrial Staplers. Even the XS-119, the self-proclaimed bad boy of the industrial stapling world has never tempted me to stray from the regulations.

"By contrast Devon in the 20th Century is a relative crime free zone, with only occasional bouts of crime brought on by holidaying Northeners and Cornish smuggling sheep over the border. Both after the riches of Devon. Devon is Gods own country and Cider gods own drink as the apple is the first fruit mentioned in the Bible. Mel. Resident of the No.1 County.

PS:good luck in Germany, I'd recommend Braunschweig as a place to visit. Best not to mention the war though."

Mel – In my mission to spread a bit of Shropshire goodness around the planet, I always want to keep the emphasis on being pro-Shropshire and not anti- Devon or anti any other county, country or continent. In saying that, it is obvious to me that any county that has "drinking apple juice" as it's main attraction need to have a good long hard look at itself in the mirror.

Mailman Joe has also been in touch, thanks for taking the time Joe. Jo had an excellent idea-

"Have you thought of campaigning for the expansion of the boundaries of Shropshire so that neighbouring counties can enjoy the benefits of being under the care of Shropshire"?

This is an inspired idea. I'm looking into the possibility of making a start on it. We could phase out Devon altogether and just have one big happy English county - Shropshire. Thank you also for congratulating me on stopping the Iraq war, though it would be remiss of me to take full credit. Before the war started, I did leave a message with Tony Blair offering to sort the whole thing out and if he got in touch all I had to do was pack my Bingo markers and I could be ready within three quarters of an hour. I think the message got a bit garbled though.

I just heard Jessica came second in the "River of Words" freeform expression category. A man called Rufus who looked a bit like Greg Dyke just sat on a stuffed Otter and chattered his teeth won first prize.

Poetry isn't what it used to be.

WEEK 23 DAY 1

The poet John Yeovil left for Shropshire today, I have sent him to explore the sensory delights of Moreton Say. I suspect when the tears of joy clear from his eyes and he is once again able to write, he will pen the most beautiful verse England has ever seen.

I'll never forget the day; it was early one morning, when the beauty of Moreton Say first really hit me. I had just finished arranging some sticklebricks into a dodecahedron and a shaft of Shropshire sunshine broke through the net curtains. I toddled over to the window and looked out to see the fields ablaze with joy. The sun was pushing over the gentle roll of the Shropshire horizon, deep hues of the morning sun's golden red mixing with the wildflowers, the trees and the rusting shell of a caravan that someone had abandoned at the bottom of our garden in

1959. I remember I felt so liberated and awakened by this glorious sight I wet myself. I was only three.

I'm in a car on my way to Frankfurt airport. I'm getting a lift from a Swedish poet called Lars Frummax who reminds me of a young Mel Croucher. Lars drives a Vauxhall Cavalier, but has painted it with flowers of many colours and written "Love" in several different languages on the bonnet. I explained to him that while I appreciate the artistic sentiment, he has significantly reduced the market value of a perfectly good car. Lars agreed with me, he was drunk and in love when he did the paint job. Now he is sober and alone the cold hard facts of the automotive sales environment have hit him and he longs for the grey metallic sheen of glory his car once knew.

He calls his car "Frans Hals". I have no idea why.

WEEK 23 DAY 2

Lars dropped me off this morning, he's off to another poetry convention in Chile - The Encuentro Internacional de Poesía. I was tempted to go with him, but I'm afraid I may become distracted with the jet set world of international poetry and neglect my responsibilities as Shropshire's ambassador of love.

Frankfurt airport looks much the same as all the other airports I've visited. Lots of planes, obviously, people looking sad waiting for their flight, sleeping stretched across three bucket seats. Why don't airports provide bunk beds in the departure area? Why do families look so miserable when they are about to go on holiday? Why don't they organise Bingo games to keep discontented travellers occupied while they wait for their plane?

Concentrating on that last question, I'm using the international language of Bingo to cheer up a group of families that were trying unsuccessfully to avoid eye contact with me. Using an airport bin as a makeshift drum, and empty cans of pop with numbers scratched on them as balls I've been able to get quite a decent game going. It's noisy but functional and I'm offering flights to Shropshire as grand prize for the first person to shout "Haus"

On the side of the bin I'm using as a drum for the numbered balls I've written Bin-go, which I thought was both funny and clever. It must have lost something in translation as not one person pointed out how amusing the pun was. I'm not sure what the German is for bingo, I do keep hearing people say "Halt's Maul" whenever I spin the bin full of old cans so perhaps that is it.

My plane is delayed. It looks like I'm joining the huddled masses in the airport departure lounge. Looks like a Shropshire style all-night Bingo session for these lucky people.

WEEK 23 DAY 3

I gave away thirteen flights to Shropshire last night. Little did the baker's dozen of winners know that I'm as much a winner as they are, that's thirteen more people that will, thanks to my machinations, bask in the radiant glory that is Shropshire.

It's a good feeling helping people. In this heartless, cold world outside Moreton Say, I've seen every side of human nature. From those that fool themselves into thinking they are happy and fulfilled even though they have never seen Shropshire, to those that are searching for Shropshire but don't know it. I've seen people whose idea of a good time is strapping themselves half-naked to a motor home wearing a magic hat, people trapped in an insular society of silly names and caravans, people working in abject misery while at the same time being contractually obliged to smile at all times and suggest fries with everything. Not once in all my travels so far have I met anyone who had the inner peace and joy, the extra choccy sprinkle of fulfilment on the cappuccino of life, the Pentium 5 smile upgrade installed on the motherboard of existence, the protective plastic of pure peace that comes with the new three piece suite of sunshine and serendipity that comes from living in the premiere English county, Shropshire.

I can't wait to bring a little of the old Shropshire magic to China.

My flight is now rescheduled to leave in two hours. Just time for a couple more games of airport bingo.

WEEK 23, DAY 4

I missed my flight due to a bit of trouble last night. An American couple called Kip and Monica took offence at my rousing game of airport Bingo and complained to airport security. Fortunately one of the winners of my flights to Shropshire was Jurgen the chief of security so his complaints were unsuccessful The problem was that Kip had a weak heart and all the stress made him go a bit giddy and he collapsed while trying to stop me spinning the Bin-go bin. This not only invalidated an exciting game that was nearing it's climax, but made me feel terribly guilty as I did grapple quite enthusiastically with him at the time.

Monica tried to stop me, but I felt it my duty to accompany Kip in the ambulance and see what I could do to help. I offered to pay their medical bills but Monica got hysterical and they had to sedate her, leaving me in charge of Kip, I had to say I was their son just to get admittance to his room. This is where the problems started, they had just hooked Kip up to a monitor when my phone went off, it was Mother ringing to tell me the grass needed cutting. The nurse heard me saying, "Not now Mother" and became suspicious because I had said Monica was my mother and she was unconscious on a hospital trolley next to me. Also, mobile phones were not allowed in the hospital and so I was taken to a small white room and told to wait.

Then Kip and Monica's real son, Chad, who looked not unlike a young Trevor Howard, turned up and I had to tell him I was his long-lost half-brother, he embraced me and we went to see our Father. Kip woke up, much shouting ensued and I slipped away in the confusion.

By the time I got back to the airport, my flight had flown. They could have waited for me.

There's a lesson to be learned here.

Not sure what it is though.

I'm booked on another flight for tomorrow.

WEEK 23 DAY 5

I decided against another session of airport bin-go. I played an arcade game – "House Of The Dead" at the airport arcade instead. It might not further my cause, but at least no one gets hurt. Unless you count the hordes of undead creatures that fell foul of my uncanny marksmanship.

My flight is boarding now, I'm sitting next to a lady who looks a bit like a cross between Kathleen Turner and a Barbary ape. Small, blonde, slightly masculine and unusually hairy. My macaque-like companion refused to give me her name and put on one of those eye-masks. I suspect she does not want to talk to me.

Still, I'm full of optimism. Finally, I'm on my way to China, land of the fortune cookie, the panda, lychees, unusually small trees, Chinese food, Chinese dragons, Chinese checkers and other things Chinese. I can't wait.

According to my travel leaflet, China is the world's fourth-largest country and considerably bigger than Shropshire with 1,284,303,705 living there. This worried me a bit, if I do manage to convince everyone in China to pop over to Shropshire the M54 might not be able to cope. The Chinese climate is apparently "extremely diverse; tropical in the south to subarctic in the north", this sounds a bit like Shropshire too, I should fit right in.

Looking out the window of the plane, we are above the clouds now. From above, the clouds look so white and pure, more solid than they should. I can imagine stepping out of the plane and going for a run in the fluffy panorama below me, it looks soft and welcoming like virgin snow. We just passed a bank of clouds that looked just like an ivory replica of the Wrekin. I told the stewardess my feelings on the cloudscape, she didn't seem very interested and just offered me some peanuts.

WEEK 23 DAY 6

It was a long flight and we have just landed in China, at the Shanghai Pudong International Airport. A lot of the people here are wearing face-masks, not sure why, perhaps the pollen count is high. The airport is all blue neon signs and white walls. There are a lot of Oriental people here.

I've booked into a hotel and want to explore Shanghai.

Shanghai is big, bigger than Oswestry, bigger even than Telford. I'm shopping now in a place called the Super Brand Mall, it's an amazingly big shopping centre, it makes Market Drayton look like a small market town. It's not what I expected at all here in China, I'd seen the Chinese television series "Monkey" at home and it's nothing like that.

I tried to speak to 27 different people today, none of them seemed to connect with me on any significant level or want to listen to things about Shropshire and how great it is. On the bright side, that still leaves 1,284,303,778 people left who might be interested in speaking to me. 16 million of them live in Shanghai, I could spend the next ten years here and only scratch the surface, I need a mass-market approach.

I went to the Chinese Communist Party Headquarters to have a word with them about the Shropshire way of life but the place was just a museum. I'm not really sure where the real seat of power is here in Shanghai, it's probably hidden somewhere but I intend to find it.

WEEK 23 DAY 7

I tried to talk to more people, not much luck. Fortunately I've got directions to a tourist company that arrange help for western visitors.

I've hired a guide, his name is Lang So Pin, he promises to help me bring Shropshire to the Chinese masses for the equivalent of £1.56 per day, not a bad deal. Lang looks a bit like an overweight Bruce Lee with bad teeth and possibly a wig. He speaks both Mandarin and standard Chinese so I hope to be able to communicate via him to most of the people I meet.

Lang tells me I should drink tea to experience the real China. I explained to him that I've been drinking tea all my life and showed him the three PG tips bags I had left in my travel pack. He laughed at me, I'm not sure why.

We are at the Hu Xin Teahouse, it's a beautiful place, all twirly banisters and knobbly roofs. They take absolutely ages making a cup of tea here. I tried to take over and use one of my last pyramid bags instead of messing around with all this loose-leaf nonsense, but they seemed quite offended so I left them to it. The cups were very small too, especially for the price they cost. I told Lang So Pin that you can have a pot of tea for one at a café in Market Drayton for 80p and get three cups out of it, he seemed suitably impressed.

Tomorrow he promises to show me the real face of Shanghai, I hope it involves Bingo.

WEEK 24 DAY 1

The more I look at it, the more Shanghai reminds me of Telford. It has many sides to it, some impressive like the Pearl Tower or Telford shopping centre; some dark and dangerous like Shanghai docks or Telford Town Park; and some just plain confusing like the Xin Cho Temple of Yangpi or that shop in Market Drayton that sells crystals and little plastic tubs with stones in them.

Lang So Pin only works as my guide five days a week, so I'm on my own for the next two days. I'm wearing my best walking shoes and striking out in downtown Shanghai on my own.

I stick out a bit, a vision of pale Shropshire man adrift in unfamiliar waters, an unfamiliar English bony bit in an Oriental processed meat sandwich.

Everyone here is shorter than me. I'm not a tall man by Moreton Say standards. Big Tom from Three Acres farm is seven foot three inches tall and his wife Big Brenda is even taller, though their unusual height is most probably a result of a childhood spent working in the radioactive wastes of Russia.

Their daughter, Big Ethel is rumoured to be taller still, but no one has seen her since she was suspended from Moreton Say Parish School for using gravestones as Frisbees. She was only seven.

I met one young woman today who did speak very good English. Her name was Julie. She told me she speaks nine different languages; I had to take her word for it. Julie looks like an oriental version of Bridget Fonda, she has that slightly psychotic twinkle in her eye that suggests she knows seventy different ways to kill a man.

Julie works at an advertising agency and seemed very keen on talking to me about my unusual life's work, so we had lunch together.

She refused to let me pay, which was nice, especially since all my money is in my left shoe and smells a bit.

It turns out that Julie is looking for a western face to feature in a new advertising campaign in Shanghai. Apparently she is trying to launch a new brand of deodorant and her company wants to do a billboard ad showing a well-groomed English gentleman as a logo for the new body spray.

The product is called "Sing-So-Min" and is specifically aimed at workers in busy and cramped offices that have to sit in close proximity with each other. I agreed to do a photo shoot for her tomorrow, she is paying me and I thought a little free publicity for my face might help me interest people in my message.

WEEK 24 DAY 2

I'm doing a photo shoot for a Chinese advertising agency today. I am the new face of "Sing-So-Min" deodorant.

They let me try the product, it comes in a brilliant container. It's an aerosol can, but it's semi-transparent so you can see the fluid inside as it goes down. It has a nozzle that looks like a chrome power shower head, only much smaller and the words "Sing-So-Min" in holographic writing around the outside. As you turn the can in your hands the letters seem to stay in the same place, while the background shifts and sparkles, it's a triumph of design.

Unfortunately the spray makes you smells like a dead badger. I pointed this out to the people taking the photos and they just gave me the thumbs up. I could see they didn't understand me, so I tried to mime it to them.

My visualisation of a badger dying was a little too graphic and before I knew it, the paramedics had been called, because they thought I was having a seizure.

Fortunately, Julie turned up and I was able to explain. I had to tell Julie that I couldn't do the photo shoot anymore. I refuse to endorse anything I have reservations about. She tried to talk me out of it and offered me money, free products and something called "Han-iti-pan", which I think is either a small fish or a moped, but I refused them all.

I am if nothing else, a man of principle.

I explained to her that the pure waters of Morris could not be contaminated with the raw sewage of commercialism, and under no circumstances would I ever give my support to anything I did not believe in.

She eventually took no for an answer, my face will not now be appearing on billboards throughout the Eastern hemisphere. I did tell Julie that if she ever wants someone to endorse any good quality stationary, an oriental version of 'Countdown' or a new Bingo Hall then she should give me a call. I gave her my number.

She didn't thank me. She seemed quite annoyed that I had backed out of our arrangement. It was probably something to do with the team of make-up artists, photographers and men in suits that had turned up to take pictures of me.

I left when she started shouting abuse at me. For someone that knows nine different languages, her choice of insults were quite pedestrian.

WEEK 24 DAY 3

Lang is back with me today, helping me decipher Shanghai.

I asked him what he did at the weekend and he said, "I practiced the Quivering Tiger". The way he said it made me not want to ask any more about how or why the tiger was quivering, so I just said, "Oh that's nice" and left it at that.

Today we are in a place called Shanghai Xintiandi. Like so much of Shanghai it consists of old buildings that have been renovated.

I asked Lang why they don't just knock them down and build new buildings instead, so he took me over to a central plaza and showed me a big plaque

– it said in several languages -

"Yesterday meets tomorrow in Shanghai today."

He said this means that keeping in touch with their history is a very important thing to the Chinese and it would be disrespectful to tear down the antique walls and tiles to replace them with plastic and concrete.

The plaque is in an area called the Shikumen buildings that used to be a residential neighbourhood dating back 300 years. The houses were built in all manner of styles because 19th century Shanghai was such a hotpot of different cultures.

The developers didn't want to lose that diversity, so they kept the exteriors and refitted all the insides with modern appliances. So basically it's like one enormous barn conversion.

Mr and Mrs Alstonefield, a lovely couple who both looked a bit like Tom Baker, once converted a barn just outside Moreton Say. It started out as a two-bedroom holiday home with a dining room, kitchen, living room and modern bathroom.

But Mr and Mrs Alstonefield decided they wanted an extra bedroom and took the unusual step of developing the property downwards and added a large bedroom in a basement they had tunnelled out of the base rock. This led them to discover a network of caves under their property and they expanded some more.

After 11 years of working on the same barn conversion they now have 19 bedrooms, five bathrooms, three kitchens, 2 living areas, a conference room, a games room, an olympic sized swimming pool, a hydroponics area, a cinema, a recording studio and a little room full of Mrs Alstonefields collection of used envelopes.

They liked the barn so much they moved in and now on the odd occasion you do see them, their skin is milky white, almost transparent and they wear large, black sunglasses.

WEEK 24 DAY 4

My guide tells me Tony Blair was in Shanghai a few days ago; I suspect he may be trying to follow me.

Tony is wanting to talk to the Chinese government about a new anti-subversion law they want to bring in that is seen as restricting free speech.

Free speech is very important to me. I demand my right to tell the world about Shropshire, so I hope they decide the new law is a bad idea.

If you are reading this Tony, feel free to contact me for any pointers on how to maintain the principles of free speech. I know you've got my number, I've left it with your office on 24 separate occasions.

I also spent some time today in an ornamental garden. It was very relaxing and quite beautiful - the attention to detail, the topiary, the delicate blooms and the obvious love and care that had gone into the garden was quite outstanding.

Not as impressive as Moreton Say the year it tried to win the 'Villages In Bloom' competition, but lovely nonetheless.

I'll never forget the sight of Old Mr Wandsworth's hedge that year, it was twenty foot high and he fashioned it into the shape of Moby Dick, with roses spouting out the airhole and a tail rimmed with violets to represent the seaspray running off the giant of the deep. He even built a crows nest on top of a nearby telegraph pole.

Mr Wandsworth dressed up as Captain Ahab and (confusing Treasure Island with Moby Dick) would sit on top of his telegraph pole shouting "Ooo-aaarr Jim Lad" at passers by. It was truly magnificent.

The only thing that let it all down was the fact that Mr Wandsworth got a little too much into character and tried to harpoon one of the Villages in Bloom judges.

WEEK 24 DAY 5

Walking around Shanghai today, people started reacting oddly to me - They would point, and a few asked for my autograph.

Now at first I thought this was normal behaviour towards a visiting envoy from an important English county. Then I noticed the things that were going on along with the pointing, like the laughing, and the holding of noses, and wafting of hands.

Lang directed my attention to a billboard hanging above us from the side of one of the larger buildings. It was a fifty-foot high photo of me surrounded by some Chinese office workers looking disgusted.

At the bottom of the image were enormous orange letters. Lang translated them for me. They said - "Do you work with a malodorous colleague? Don't smell like dead animal, use Sing-So-Min for freshness and confidence."

I am now known throughout Shanghai as the man who smells like a dead animal. It's not really the image I was going for, and they used my photos even after I expressed my misgivings about Sing-So-Min.

Perhaps I shouldn't have signed all those forms that Julie gave me.

WEEK 24 DAY 6

With the help of my guide, translator and friend, I was able to give a small speech in one of Shanghai's busy market squares today.

I had to speak slowly so Lang could keep up. He had some difficulty in translating the odd phrase, "damping the fires of evil with my hose of truth" proved particularly confusing for him, and a few of my audience tried to set fire to me with their cigarette lighters, so I think they missed the point along there somewhere.

The crowd got a bit ugly towards the end of my speech and Lang made me leave. Apparently the regime in China doesn't take too kindly to free expression, but I explained to Lang that I am not afraid to face the authorities.

Sometimes you have to awaken the sleeping dragon to find out what it really thinks. Maybe the Chinese government are just ready for a few fresh ideas and no one has had the courage to tell them about places like Shropshire where everything works really well and everyone is happy.

After the potential violence, my guide Lang has offered to show me a few of the hidden secrets of hand-to-hand combat. I wanted an early night and a nice hot bath so I arranged for him to start my instruction tomorrow.

WEEK 24 DAY 7

Lang is trying to teach me some Chinese Martial arts today.

I did tell him that I had some rudimentary skills in the deadly art of Kung-Fu; I neglected to tell him that this knowledge consisted mostly of watching Hong Kong Phooey after school every Wednesday.

All the things that Lang-So-Pin is teaching me seem to have animalistic names.

Apparently The Crane, The Crouching Beetle, The Preying Mantis, The Bobbing Vole, The Wobbling Cobra, The Dancing Pony and The Burrowing Terrapin are all going to become part of my deadly repertoire.

Despite his portly outward appearance, Lang is surprisingly nimble. I saw him do a back-flip over a small fence, a high kick that knocked the glass from a streetlight, and he folded a small piece of card into a little swan whose wings flap when you pull its legs.

I was very impressed.

WEEK 25 DAY 1

Now that Lang is showing me some basic moves, I have to call him "Sensei Pin".

This in itself didn't bother me, but after several hours of grinding my knuckles in a bucket of sand to harden them and then being made to sleep at the foot of Lang's bed in a small cage, I feel the employer/employee relationship has changed somewhat.

I only wanted to learn how to look threatening and then run away but Lang seems intent on turning me into his prodigy.

When I find the appropriate moment I'll explain to him that I am a man of peace and I don't see how hitting and kicking people will convince them to move to Shropshire.

Violence is never the answer. Unless of course the question is "Think of a word that rhymes with fence and starts with 'V', or "What is Vinnie Jones famous for?", or "What is Ecneloiv spelled backwards?".

Violence is hardly ever the answer.

WEEK 25 DAY 2

I'm on a 24 hour a day training schedule. I haven't worked this hard since Aunt Felicity sprained her ankle on the top of the Wrekin and I had to carry her home.

Lang is a harsh master. Every time I try to tell him that I want to stop doing the Pouncing Leopard and start doing the Sleeping Morris he prods me with a stick and shouts at me in Mandarin.

I am bruised, tired and sore, but I must admit I do feel fitter and stronger than I ever have before. My muscles are firm and my head is clear.

I've been put on a strict diet of water and rice, though I have been able to supplement this with some gingerbread I had hidden in my bag, and by sucking on a copy of "War Poems of Wilfred Owen" that I spilled Ribena over while I was in Holland. It still retains a blackcurrenty flavour and hopefully some vitamin C content .

WEEK 25 DAY 3

Sensei Pin has an extensive library of books on the martial arts.

I am permitted three hours at night to study these texts. They are really quite fascinating. I'm looking through them to see if I can find anything to support my theory that martial arts originated in Shropshire.

WEEK 25 DAY 4

I'm actually getting quite interested in this whole martial arts thing.

In much the same way Bruce Lee took aspects of different martial arts to create Jeet Kune Do, I want to meld judo , kendo, karate, wing chun, arnis, silat, kung-fu throw in a bit of Japanese Bujitsu, and the Kalaripayattu of India and develop a new Shropshire-inspired martial art based on a hybrid of all these teachings, but concentrating more on the running away bit.

I shall call it "The Way Of The Badger".

WEEK 25 DAY 5

I had a phone call from Julie today. She was incredibly apologetic for the way she acted before.

Apparently the advertising campaign that features my photo and something about me smelling like a dead animal has become a massive hit. She wants me to feature in a series of television adverts.

I told her that there were two very good reasons why I could not feature in a series of television adverts.

Firstly, I explained to her again that it would be against my principles to endorse a product I did not think highly of. If people see me as someone who supports an inferior product for personal gain, they may mistake my championing of Shropshire as insincere, and that would be terrible.

Secondly, I'm currently chained to a cage while an aging, overweight master of the martial arts tries to turn me into Shropshire's answer to Jon Claude Van Damme.

The Fists of Clay from Moreton Say .

WEEK 25 DAY 6

I tried yet again today to tell Sensei Pin that I don't want to be a one man death machine.

He just smiled peacefully and went on and on about how his teachings are not about death; they are about life, inner peace, tranquillity that sort of thing.

If it's all so tranquil, why do I spend all day hitting and kicking things?

WEEK 25 DAY 7

Today I am permitted a 12 hour respite from my training schedule.

I shall be using this time to contemplate the things I have learned, rest a little and then to escape over the fence and run like the wind.

I've left Lang a note telling him he is fired. I gave him a months salary and an open invitation to Moreton Say, no hard feelings.

China is, I've decided, a difficult place to spread my particular Salopian message. The natives are not only suspicious generally of anything Western, they are doubly suspicious of the man from the "smells like a dead animal" advertisements trying to convince them about lifestyle changes.

However, Shropshire comes with me wherever I go, both literally and figuratively. I carry some of my homeland's soil (from my Mother's garden in Moreton Say) in my pocket and I carry the intangible hopes and ideals distilled by the generations who have lived in Shropshire.

I still see a lot of potential here in China and I'm travelling north to see if I have more success in rural China.

I no longer have a guide to help me speak the language and show me around, but I have bought a phrasebook, some new trousers and I am in better shape physically than I've ever been, so I'm optimistic I can do some good somewhere.

I just hope Lang doesn't follow me.

WEEK 26 DAY 1

In the fine tradition of John Inman, I'm free!

Unfettered by the constraints of my over-zealous tour-guide/sensei, I am walking through the suburbs of Shanghai and into the increasingly wild countryside of China.

I don't have a map, or indeed the slightest clue where I am going. But I do know one thing - wherever I go I'll tell people about my beloved homeland, I'll sing from the rooftops about the marvels of Moreton Say and whenever possible educate, liberate and motivate using the ideals and values I learned growing up in the finest county on earth.

I may not be able to convince the entire population of China to relocate to the grassy slopes and good life of Shropshire, but I'm going to give it a jolly good try.

I talked to a mother and her child as they sat by the roadside today. They didn't know any English, but they did recognise me from the deodorant advert I inadvertently appeared in.

The child held its nose and pointed at me with unrestrained glee. I tried to use my English/Chinese phrasebook but it proved essentially useless.

Phrasebooks are always full of exactly the sort of things I don't want to say. I don't want to ask where the airport is, I don't want to order from the menu, and I have no intention of asking for my steak medium rare or inquiring if someone could pass the salt. I just want to tell people about Shropshire.

I settled for drawing that most beautiful of polygons, the outline of Shropshire, in dirt, with a stick. They both looked singularly unimpressed. You never know though, when that child grows up, they may be haunted by the residual image of Shropshire's borders and endeavour to seek out some meaning in the image.

Eventually this can only bring them to the hallowed ground and only good can come of that. I've always found the shape of Shropshire to be incredibly pleasing to the eye.

I can honestly say that I'd rather ponder the curves and corners of a perfectly scaled map of Shropshire's borders than I would the curves of a gorgeous woman's body, the delicate brush stokes of a renaissance master or the mathematically intriguing lines of Carol Voderman's instep.

I'm sure I'm not the only one who feels this way. In fact if you stare at the shape of Shropshire for long enough, and when I say long enough I mean a good 74 hour stretch, it looks almost exactly like a woman in flowing robes, opening her arms in a gesture of nurture and peace, or sometimes it looks like an elephant with two legs missing, no trunk and a little hat with a peacock feather in it, or a sort of special machine for measuring how long a biscuit can be safely dunked in a cup of tea for and once I thought it looked like a thousand spinning faces, all staring and laughing and shouting over and over again in a macabre choir of mockery – "Morris, Morris, Girly Florist".

WEEK 26 DAY 2

I'm walking the B-roads of China, searching for someone who needs my own peculiar brand of help. Ideally, someone who is feeling repressed and trodden upon by the Chinese regime and is open to the idea of relocation to the West Midlands, or a small community prepared to declare themselves part of Shropshire.

At the moment I'd settle for helping someone across the road, or buying someone a nice cup of tea and a scone.

I haven't met anyone for a few hours now. This morning I did pass an old man pulling an ancient wooden rickshaw behind him. He was leathered and weary with age, like a walnut with a manic grin and two suspicious eyes.

I asked him what he was pulling on such a hot and dry day in the middle of nowhere. He whipped the tarpaulin off his cargo with a magician's flourish to reveal a rickshaw full of DVDs, all with the photocopied covers, familiar to anyone who has frequented car-boot sales.

The man's name, I think, was Rasputin, not a typical Chinese name as far as I'm aware.

Rasputin's broken English suggested he makes quite a tidy living selling DVD's to the comparatively wealthy occupants of Shanghai.

The odd thing was, the pirated films were primarily Doris Day movies. Apparently Doris is very popular in China, she embodies the spirit of purer times. Times before John Woo started putting people's pistols in both hands at once and when bursting into song was far more likely than bursting someone's stomach open with an automatic weapon.

Rasputin must have had over 1000 copies of "That Touch Of Mink" stacked up in his makeshift vehicle, with a few hundred "Please Don't Eat The Daisies", a box of "On Moonlight Bay", another box of "Pillow Talk" and a bundle of "Last of The Mohicans".

I pointed out to Rasputin that "Last of The Mohicans" was Daniel Day-Lewis, not Doris Day but he wouldn't have it, he kept pointing to the poorly photocopied picture of Daniel in full-on red Indian regalia, stabbing it with his finger and firmly saying "Doris, Doris".

I relented, agreed it was Doris after all and pointed out how good she was looking for her age, this seemed to please him.

Before he left, I shared with him what I had left of some rice crackers I'd bought in Shanghai. He gave me a copy of "With Six You Get Eggroll" as a gift and I accepted it, not because I wanted to, or indeed was able to watch it, but because it was given in simple gratitude and it would have been impolite to refuse his kindness.

I still gave him a good talking to about the dangers of media piracy; how it is essentially stealing from the artist by depriving them of any royalties they might get from a legitimate copy.

He seemed genuinely hurt that what he was doing could be seen as stealing from Doris Day and he left me promising to give his profession some serious thought.

WEEK 26 DAY 3

I read today that some Chinese geneticists have engineered a human/rabbit hybrid. Not so very far from where I am now they are playing with the building blocks of life.

Apparently the hybrid is not permitted to grow to full-term but it still makes me hopping mad that they are experimenting with such dangerous concoctions.

We have a lot of rabbits in Moreton Say and I know from bitter childhood experience that they can breed at an alarming rate. I once let Fluffy rabbit sleep over with Peter rabbit and within the space of three months there were so many new bunnies, I actually ran out of amusing names for them all.

My Mother wanted to have them destroyed but fortunately I was 27 and able to overpower my Mother long enough to find them all good homes.

Imagine if just a couple of these human/rabbit hybrids escaped the Chinese laboratory? Within the year China could be overrun with buck toothed, big eared, fluffy, six feet tall monsters eating all the carrots and leaving droppings on the carpet.

WEEK 26 DAY 4

I met a young man called Jun Shan today. He was the only person I passed on the road that admitted to speaking any English.

I suspect a few of the people I approached knew full well what I was saying to them but feigned ignorance. I seem to get that a lot in foreign countries.

Jun is travelling on foot, like myself, but heading the opposite way, towards Shanghai.

Jun comes from a small village in central China called Ten-Po-Xia and he describes it with such enthusiasm. I promised to visit it if I pass that way. He tells me that in Ten-Po-Xia the people are like one big happy family, they all share their good fortune with each other, they are always polite and they never play loud music after 9pm.

Jun wants to travel the world telling everyone about Ten-Po-Xia, he doesn't understand why everyone can't just be like the people in his village and just get on with each other and be nice all of the time.

Jun is clearly a bit mad. I set him straight and gave him directions to Moreton Say.

WEEK 26 DAY 5

I came across a temple today, a lovely old building with a twiddly roof, very Chinese looking.

A man in a blue coat was sitting outside, presumably waiting for it to open and thumbing through a dog-eared copy of the I-Ching.

The man was very sage-like; he did that thing where he paused for three or four minutes before answering any of my questions or responding in any way.

Like this –

"Hello", I said.

Three minute pause.

"Hello" he replied.

"Nice Day." I said.

Three minute pause.

"Might rain" he replied.

I would have said something in the gap but he always looked like he was just on the verge of saying something.

I used to know a farmer that communicated like this, he was called Clive. I don't really know much else about Clive, I could never be bothered to hang around long enough to find out.

After a frustrating half hour of stilted pleasantries and in anticipation of the pauses, I asked the man in the blue coat a multi-level question –

"Is the temple open, if so what time does it open, what happens inside, do they welcome westerners and can I interest you in learning about Shropshire?"

Three minute pause.

"The less trodden path is often so full of stones, it is better to make a new path. But the wise traveller waits at the crossroads for the destination to come to him." he replied.

I thanked him and left.

I wish people would just give a straight answer without just trying to be all inscrutable and mysterious.

In Moreton Say we get straight to the point like a willow arrow, shot from the steely arm of a master marksman; a soaring eagle descending on a field mouse that it spotted from three miles up; a dart arcing with pinpoint accuracy from the chubby clamp of Jockey Wilson's fist into the double 19 match point winning the tournament.

I hate it when people beat around the bush like that.

WEEK 26 DAY 6

Mother called.

I haven't spoken to her for quite some time, nearly a week now, and she was full of news.

Aunt Felicity was arrested again for stubbing out a cigar on a policeman. Toby and Sophia are redecorating the house next door; they are spending more time in what they call a 'love-nest' in the back garden where they apparently go out to on the warmer evenings for romantic liaisons.

Mother is disgusted at this blatant exhibitionism. She told me that if she stands on the edge of the bath and leans out the upper window holding a shaving mirror in her outstretched arm, she can clearly see right into the love-nest.

She misses me and asked me to come home again, emphasising again her inability to cope with the garden without me.

I told her, as usual, that I have yet to, and may never, complete my journey, my quest, my calling to tell the world about Shropshire.

The flame of burning desire that wills me on has not dimmed, it burns still brighter as if fed by a combination of barbeque lighter fluid, petrol and really good quality charcoal, the extra-long burning sort that has the firelighter compound built into the bricks themselves.

I'll be the first to admit that China has not so far provided the ripest of crops in terms of people wanting to live the Shropshire way, but I did build a little pile of rocks by the road today and made a sign on top of it pointing westwards saying "Moreton Say - 8536 miles".

WEEK 26 DAY 7

A quiet day on the road today.

I've been walking for a week now and must have made some considerable distance from Shanghai.

I can't see much in the way of civilisation anywhere on the horizon, which is fine. It reminds me of the peace and open spaces of Moreton Say, only with less sheep and more pagodas.

I slept for quite a bit, lying on a small hill that overlooked the roadside. I was a bit bored, so I tore some leaves into the shape of Shropshire and put them on my bare chest when I went to sleep.

When I woke up the sun had burned the outline of the motherland betwixt my nipples, it looks very special.

WEEK 27 DAY 1

Rasputin passed me again today, with his rickshaw full of pirated DVDs.

He took great pride in showing me the contents of his rickshaw. No longer does it contain illicit Doris Day movies, it is now filled to the very brim with copied Billy Crystal films.

His reasoning is that while he venerates Doris Day and would never want to steal from her, he dislikes Billy Crystal immensely and quite likes the idea of ripping him off. Not really the result I was looking for when I chastised him last week for selling pirated films, but his heart is in the right place - his decision was motivated by his love for Doris and I didn't have the heart to complain to him anymore.

The worst thing about it all is I feel responsible now for subjecting the population of Shanghai to multiple copies of City Slickers One and Two. No one deserves that.

WEEK 27 DAY 2

I left the beaten track today and headed into the wilderness.

I've hardly met anyone on the roads of China, so I'm thinking everyone must live off-road. I'm going looking for them.

I've been walking for four hours now, my legs are cut from the unusually aggressive Chinese bushes, and the weather is taking a turn for the worse. Not so long ago it was quite sunny and pleasant. Then the wind picked up about half an hour ago and rain keeps coming down in quick bursts, like someone throwing cold buckets of water over me and then running away.

The wind makes my soaked clothes feel like a coat made from needles of ice. I think maybe this is what they mean by Chinese water torture.

To keep the cold at bay I'm trying singing old Moreton Say folk songs. I've forgotten most of the words to "Shropshire Bob And Keith His Giant Dog", but old favourites like "We'll Be Digging Up Potatoes Till We Bleed" and "The Vicar Lost His Temper In The Pub Last Night" are not easily forgotten.

Singing helps keep my spirits up and should frighten away any wild animals. I'm not sure what wild animals they have in China. I'm pretty sure the dragons are fictitious and I'm confident I can outrun a panda, but I have a nagging memory of reading about something with large, sharp teeth and a bad attitude that lives in China - was it a tiger? Or a really big rodent of some sort? I can't remember.

It might just be the cold and exhaustion playing tricks with my mind, but I keep thinking I can hear my Mother calling to me, willing me to come home where it's warm, it's safe, there's a plentiful supply of Jammie Dodgers and I can watch Countdown in my dressing gown.

Still wet, very cold.

Going to try and get some sleep, I've found a hollow in some rock. I say hollow, it's too slight to call a cave, more of a dent in the rock, but it offers a little protection from the elements. I'm curling up here for the night. I hope it's nicer tomorrow and I meet some people who speak English and have an easily stimulated desire to learn about Shropshire.

WEEK 27 DAY 3

I woke up this morning at sunrise.

Generally I would turn over and go back to sleep at this hour, but instead of a sleepmaster 3000 orthopaedic mattress and my Star Wars duvet cover, my bed consists of a hard, cold, wet hollow in a rock face, so I've decided to get up early.

Nothing to eat for breakfast. I looked around for some nuts and berries. I didn't find any. If you ever go camping in the Chinese wilderness, I'd recommend taking a sturdy packed lunch.

Wherever I am it is all hard soil and spiky bushes, nothing to eat, nothing to see, no one to talk to.

It's a bit like what I imagine Devon must be like.

WEEK 27 DAY 4

I'm getting a bit worried now. Haven't seen anyone or indeed anything for what seems like a lifetime.

It's only actually been a couple of days, so it's not really been a lifetime, unless I was a fruit fly, or my metabolism was wildly accelerated so I lived out my life in two days, but then I'd be able to run really, really fast and could find somewhere nice a lot quicker.

I tried to ring someone but I can't get my phone to work. I don't know where I am in China, my feet are sore and I haven't had a decent game of Bingo in ages.

I feel quite peculiar.

WEEK 27 DAY 5

Today I fixed my eyes on a single point on the horizon and headed straight for it.

I reasoned that this way I could cover the most ground and would reach civilisation a lot quicker.

What I really want to do is go back the way I came and find the road, but I don't know which way that is, so in the circumstances one direction is as good as another.

I seem to be walking upwards quite a lot; it's actually getting quite difficult to keep climbing. I think the point on the horizon I was fixing on might have been the top of a mountain, and if the terrain gets any harder I'll have to pick another focal point.

It's still very windy. I can see why kites are so popular in China. I had a kite once, back in Moreton Say, when life was simple and non-threatening. It was blue and red with a picture of a rabbit on it. One windy Shropshire evening I went into the fields to fly it and tripped over a real rabbit, let go of the cord, and never saw it again.

Since then, I've always associated rabbits with kites, although they actually have very little in common. Squirrels are an animal more suited to kite association.

WEEK 27 DAY 6

For the first time since I set out on a one man odyssey to right wrongs and get the whole world Shropshire-bound, I feel like I might not make it any further.

I'm so high up now, the air is noticeably thinner. I find myself panting like old Farmer Wentworth's sheepdog, Frummax, used to when you waved a Cornetto at him.

I'm going to have little lie down, there's a shiny light in the sky and I think it's calling my name.

WEEK 27 DAY 7

Yesterday I thought I was going to go to the big Bingo Hall in the sky, but once again the kindly fingers of fate have snatched me from the very tonsils of despair and deposited me in the ample bosoms of opportunity.

I was lying on the side of a mountain, frost was gathering on my face and I was wondering how long it had been since I last breathed, when a little bald man put me over his shoulder and brought me here.

I'm in what I suppose is a guest room in a monastery full of Ch'an sect Shaolin monks. Fifty of them live in isolation here, in a building hewn from the base rock of the mountain itself. They keep telling me they are waiting, but I'm not sure what it is they are waiting for exactly.

I've only had chance to talk a little to the monks. They have encouraged me to spend some time in contemplative concentration. They say I need to rest after my ordeal.

Apparently when the monk found me on the mountain, he thought I was dead - my pulse had stopped, I was stiff as a board and ice cold.

He brought me up to the monastery and was looking through my belongings to identify the body when he read out the name tag on my anorak - "Morris Telford, Shropshire". When I heard the word Shropshire, I snapped to life again just like someone had plugged me back in. I gave the little, bald monk a nasty shock.

They warmed me up in a big metal bath, gave me some robes and put me in here with my belongings and a tray of little biscuits that are reminiscent of Market Drayton gingerbread.

The monastery has been here since 500 AD, but they are surprisingly well-equipped. I notice the room I'm in, although bare with a stone floor, has a phone socket and a mini-bar.

Someone is coming.

It was the little, bald monk who found me. His name, I found out after a little confusion, is So.

So looks like a bald version of Barney Rubble; he even sounds just like him. I asked him to say "Hey, Fred" a few times and it was very funny indeed.

So is the cobbler for the monastery. He mends all the shoes with a needle and fine wire, so So sews shoes.

He strikes me as a bit odd, but then who isn't?

So told me about a prophesy the Kung-Fu soldier monks up here have passed down for 1500 years. When they are not performing extraordinary feats of discipline, strength and courage they are waiting for the "frozen stranger to die and live again." According to the prophesy, he will lead them to "a golden land of eternal peace".

Sounds like they've been waiting for me. I can't wait to enlighten them with tales of Moreton Say.

WEEK 28 DAY 1

I slept really well last night, better than I have since I set out from Shropshire to change the world.

I woke up with that feeling that I could tackle absolutely anything that the world could possibly throw at me!

It may be that I have finally found a whole community of people ready to accept everything I have to teach them about doing things the Shropshire way. It may be that after so long travelling, I have reached a place where people appreciate me. It may be that coming here has re-affirmed my self-belief and given me new vigour in my quest to change the world.

Or it may be that I slept so well because of the bed of flower petals and multi-coloured feathers sprinkled with incense and fragrant oils that the monks prepared for me; the constantly replenished supply of freshly-drawn mountain spring water; the exotic selection of peeled fruits within easy reach of my bed; and the gentle playing of the mandolin from the monk perched on my balcony.

Whatever it was, I slept the sleep of the just and I feel fully prepared for the meeting I have with the assembly of Shaolin monks at noon today.

Some of the monks actually avert their eyes when I walk by, I asked about this and it's a form of reverence and not, as I first presumed, because I am visually offensive to them.

WEEK 28 DAY 2

The meeting went well yesterday. They gave me an orange ankle-length robe to wear, and at my request they sewed the shape of Shropshire into the back of it in green silk. I hope they let me keep it.

The prophesy of the "frozen stranger" required me to give the monks a task as a test of their obedience and loyalty. I had wanted them all to travel to Shropshire straight away but on reflection, I saw an opportunity for genuine progression of my cause and gave them a task equal to their not inconsiderable abilities.

I asked the monks to build me an exact replica of Moreton Say. Basing the design on my instructions, sketches and a few photos I have left of me, they are going to recreate the splendour of the little Shropshire village I was born in. But this time

Moreton Say is not going to rest secure in the heart of Shropshire, this new Moreton Say nestles on the remote mountain slopes of China, a beacon of hope for any travellers in search of a new life.

The monks began work yesterday straight after I spoke to them all and I must say they are very keen. They have already shown me detailed plans for a reasonable facsimile of my house and Sophia's house and are beginning work on a scale model of the parish church.

A party of twenty monks have been sent down the mountain to find out about getting some tarmac for the main road and the blacksmith monk is working hard on some authentic road signs - it's all very exciting.

There is even talk of a bio-dome to recreate the climatic conditions of Shropshire and some of the younger boy monks are now being trained daily in speaking English in a fluent Shropshire accent (You too could learn to speak Salop!).

I asked them for a projected finish date this morning and they have just got back to me now as I sit in my room watching the sun set over the snow-capped peaks outside. They estimate that they will have a life-size copy of Moreton Say up and running by the end of August 2008.

It's a bit longer than I expected but apparently a deadline is a very important thing to a monk and they ensure me that on 31/08/2008 and not a day later, a large chunk of the mountain range will be virtually indistinguishable from Shropshire.

If I'd known I was committing the whole community of monks to five years hard labour I might just have asked for a painting of Moreton Say instead, or a nice tapestry, but what's done is done and they all seem very happy to have such a big project to work on.

I've given them meaning in their lives, and that surely is the greatest gift you can give anyone. The monks refuse to let me help them in anything but a supervisory capacity, which while an important position, makes me feel a bit useless. I like to be actually doing things and as anyone who has ever worked in an office will tell you, from middle management upwards, no one actually does anything.

Managers go to meetings and talk about other people doing things. They make long lists of action points, action plans, action mapping exercises and other things beginning in 'action' to try and fool you into thinking something, somewhere must be getting done. In fact they haven't achieved anything in decades and have only a very cloudy idea of what it is they are supposed to be managing.

I don't want to be like that, I want to do things.

Perhaps I'm being over-ambitious, but since the monks are doing such a sterling job of recreating the idyllic locale of Moreton Say, I'm wondering if I shouldn't get them to keep going beyond 2008. Build a replica of the A road to Market Drayton, then a replica of Market Drayton itself, then Longford, Ternhill, Marchamley, then even Telford and on and on until the whole of Shropshire is recreated in the Chinese mountain ranges.

I was thinking this over, but then I saw that a couple of the monks had already collapsed from exhaustion and thought better of mentioning my ideas for further expansion just yet.

WEEK 28 DAY 3

Today I'm overseeing the beginning of some foundation building work of New Moreton Say.

My team of kung-fu warrior monks are flouting Health and Safety laws and not wearing hardhats on site, but since most of them can break bricks with their foreheads anyway they are probably in less danger of cranial injury than most building site workers.

My mother had some builders round in 1998 to build a new porch for us. I remember there were three of them and they all wore bobble hats and smelled of prunes.

They started work on the Tuesday, tore down the old porch with great enthusiasm and made a little knee-high wall of bricks in a vaguely porch-like outline. Then they went home with their 30 percent deposit and we never saw them again.

I related this anecdote to the monks this morning and before I could stop them, seven trained assassin monks had been dispatched to hunt down the three men and bring them to justice for stealing from the family of the frozen stranger. So if you are reading this and happen to be a builder in the Shropshire area, I'd advise against wearing hats with bobbles on or eating dried fruit.

Given that this is a five-year project I broke the news to them earlier that I'm going to pop out for a few years and come back when it's finished.

They didn't take this terribly well. There was a great deal of wailing, beating of brows and tearing of undergarments, but fortunately as the prophetic frozen stranger I wield supreme authority and they were soon making travel arrangements for me.

I've left So in charge, and they have my phone number if they need to ring me about anything.

WEEK 28 DAY 4

The Shaolin monks made an enormous fuss when I left.

I got out of bed at sunrise and it was getting dark by the time all the music, banners, displays of martial arts, singing, plate balancing, novelty acts and heartfelt reading of the prophesy of the frozen stranger had finished.

I promised to return in five years and lead my people to the golden land. I've put it in my Palmtop calender so I won't forget. August 31, 2008 = "Alert- Remember to return to China, inspect New Moreton Say and lead Shaolin Monks to the golden land."

I asked them not to follow me but as I sit in my sleeping bag here on the mountainside I can see flashes of orange robe all over the shop.

WEEK 28 DAY 5

I woke up this morning and found myself being carried along on a sort of stretcher by a team of eight monks.

Considering my every word is supposed to be obeyed, I asked them why they disobeyed me and followed me, they quite rightly pointed out that they were not following me, they were carrying me, so I sat back and enjoyed the ride.

I'm sitting back now, bobbing along the road to Shanghai, it's very nice. An old woman was sitting by the side of the road so I got the monks to lower me to the ground. She seemed upset and I enquired why.

Apparently she is a big Doris Day fan and the only source of Doris Day DVDs in the whole of China has suddenly dried up. I felt responsible so I asked the monks to give her a lift home and she cheered up quite a bit. As they raised her onto their shoulders she was warmly grinning and clutching a copy of "Throw Momma from the Train".

It's not far to Shanghai now so I'm walking the rest of the way .

WEEK 28 DAY 6

I notice that Sir Funkalot has left a message for me on the BBC boards suggesting I visit Japan.

Since China is well under way to becoming the next Shropshire, it seems like a capital idea to try my hand at the land of the rising sun, so I've booked a flight to Japan.

At the travel agents I met two American men, Vince and Drew. Vince looks like a young Jon Pertwee, but with twice the nose, and Drew bears a quite startling resemblance to David Blaine, only without the glass box surrounding him.

Drew and Vince got talking to me about my one man journey of enlightenment. I told them about the monks I've been staying with and they seemed sceptical, but nonetheless we went to have a coffee together at an Internet Café in Shanghai.

They work in the "IT business". I explained to them that I have extensive experience in lower level consumable procurement myself and we had an ever so nice chat about recent innovations in laser printer technology and toner quality.

Vince and Drew were very helpful yesterday. They gave me all sorts of tips on how to raise my profile. They applauded me (literally, they stood up and both clapped with genuine glee in quite a camp fashion) for getting my daily journals on the BBC Shropshire website, but they encouraged me to branch out into merchandising.

I'm not so sure myself. I noticed as they left me today that Vince was wearing a watch on both wrists, I don't know why but this troubled me.

WEEK 28 DAY 7

Vince and Drew were very helpful yesterday and today they went to the trouble of setting up an online store for me.

I sat with them in the Internet café and helped with some of the designs. I'm very happy with the "I LOVE SHROPSHIRE" lunchbox (my idea), but I have a few reservations about the "VISIT MORETON SAY" boxer shorts (Drew's idea).

They are available to buy at www.cafepress.com/morristelford. All proceeds go to helping make the world one big Shropshire, and maybe help me replenish my bingo marker collection.

My plane leaves for Japan tonight.

WEEK 29 DAY 1

Busy day today.

Flew with Air China overnight to terminal two of Narita Airport. I sat next to a young Japanese boy who did nothing but play on a Gameboy Advance for the entire trip. This was doubly irritating in that he didn't respond to anything I said to him and he didn't let me have a go on Mega Man Battle Network 3.

I had the usual hearty welcome at customs. Why is it every time I pass through customs and they ask me my reason for visiting the country they will never accept the truth.

I'm not coming for business reasons or pleasure reasons. I'm visiting the country to try and tell the people all about Shropshire and perhaps convince a few to relocate or at least embrace the Shropshire way of life. It's not complicated; I just want to make people happy, so why do I always come up against this scepticism with airport security the world over?

I tried to give one of the guards a little A5 brochure I had about Shropshire, nothing divisive just a picture of Moreton Say, a few paragraphs about how nice Shropshire is, my Mother's home address and a voucher entitling you to 20p off a toasted teacake at a café in Market Drayton and he accused me of offering him a bribe. It's so hard to convince people that I don't have any ulterior motive; I do hope the rest of Japan is less cautious in accepting my help.

After some confusion at the check in over why exactly I was in Japan, they did let me go and I managed to get a bus to Tokyo. The bus was very clean and pleasant, without the odour of urine I am accustomed to on British transport.

First impressions of Japan, it's very nice. I'm staying in a tall, gleaming steel and glass hotel - it looks a bit like my Mother's old greenhouse, only bigger and with rooms and guests instead of tomatoes and the engine from a 1976 Mini.

There seems to be a lot of American businessmen here, so there's a lot of speaking slowly and shouting going on in reception.

The Japanese staff are very polite and their English is excellent, I asked one of the women at reception about local Bingo halls and she was most enthusiastic and helpful, giving me a long list of local establishments. I think I'm going to like Japan.

WEEK 29 DAY 2

Walking round Tokyo today was a revelation. Everyone is so polite - not polite in a "come in and tell us all about Shropshire" kind of way, more in an "avoid eye contact with the odd looking Englishman" type manner. But at least no one has kidnapped me, drugged me, venerated me or strapped me to the top of a Winnebago.

I talked to a group of young men outside an arcade, they seemed disinterested at first while I told them about Shropshire, but when I mentioned I'd spent the last week with Shaolin monks it got their attention.

Apparently they are a street gang called the Yumo-Ka-Tekk-Boyz, which as far as I could tell is like a Japanese equivalent of the Boy Scouts. But instead of knowing hundreds of ways to tie a knot, they pride themselves on their martial arts prowess.

Fresh from my training in China, I may have overstated my own ability and ended up agreeing to take part in a contest of champions in two days. They seemed friendly enough about it though so I'm sure it's all in good fun, they gave me a blue scarf to wear tied to my arm to signify I was one of their organisation.

I agreed to see them in a couple of days at somewhere called the Tako-Do arena and left them to help old people across the road.

Watched TV in my hotel room. No sign of Countdown or its Japanese equivalent, but I did find a game show where the contestants have to put themselves through all sorts of obscure mental tortures to score points... so I settled for that instead.

WEEK 29 DAY 3

I saw some Japanese fighting fish in Tokyo today. I used to have a goldfish called Dave Ottley. He was named after Dave Ottley from Telford who won a silver medal for the javelin in the 1985 Olympics. Dave (the man not the fish) is now Sports Development Officer for Wrekin District Council but can still skewer a tangerine from 500 paces.

The Japanese fighting fish made my goldfish Dave look like just a harmless pet, which, of course, he was. The fighting fish were kept one per tank and just hovered in the centre. They didn't swim around or practice their fighting moves, or leap majestically from the tank or anything; they just floated at a stationary point in the centre of each tank and waited.

There was also a really unpleasant smell around the fish, a stinky, rotten, decaying, fetid smell. It may have been the fish, it may have been the man selling the fish, I'm not sure which.

I asked the man with the fish, who I noticed had plasters on each of his fingers, why they don't move. He told me, in an authentic accent, "they are preparing for battle". I'm ashamed to say that I laughed at the man when he said this.

The prospect of these little fish doing anything resembling "battle" struck me as absurd. My laughter did not go down well with the little Japanese fish selling man and he started shouting about the ancient art of Japanese fish fighting, the sacred history of fighting fish breeding going back centuries and something about western ignorance. He then dared me to put my hand in the tank.

In retrospect, sitting here at the Tokyo Medical and Surgical Clinic in Kamiya-cho with my hand in tatters, putting it in the tank was a bad idea.

WEEK 29 DAY 4

It's the martial arts tournament today and I'm going to the Tako-Do arena to explain I will be unable to represent my Boy Scout friends as a vicious fish attacked me yesterday.

The collection of youths waiting for me at the arena did not seem to be taking my fish wound seriously and I noticed that the majority of them seemed to be wearing red bandanas, headbands, scarves or other garments that clashed quite obviously with my blue scarf.

Also in the background I could see some quite violent confrontations going on, not at all the sort of thing Lord Baden-Powell would have approved of.

When I was a young man in Moreton Say we never had anything like this. We never used to attack each other or feel a need to separate ourselves into gangs.

I say "we", but to be fair the only friends I ever really associated with in Moreton Say that were under 25 were both made of straw. I still have very fond memories of those lazy summer days in the sun-drenched fields with my friends, Tony the scarecrow and wicker Amy, and they both taught me a very important lesson about never playing with matches.

What with all the shouting and fighting and fish bite belittling, I didn't much like the look of Tako-Do arena so I practiced what I consider to be the foundation teaching of Salopian martial arts, I ran away. It's often the bravest thing to do.

WEEK 29 DAY 5

I met a man called Yoshi today in the business district of Tokyo. He was sitting on a metal bench in a smart suit and tie eating a bowl of what looked like, and indeed turned out to be, raw fish.

Yoshi was very receptive to my tales of Shropshire life. I sat next to him on the bench and talked to him for nearly two hours, covering most of the basics about how nice it is in Shropshire and including a few personal anecdotes about amusing country happenings involving tractors, small animals and crop drainage.

It was after talking to him for a couple of hours, I asked him if I was making him late for work. This turned out to be a crucial question. Yoshi broke down - not in great big sobbing floods of tears or anything, like you do when you first find out as a young boy that London is the capital city of Great Britain and not in fact Oswestry like your Mother told you, but a restrained anguish of self-hugging and rocking back and forth.

It turned out that Yoshi lost his job last year. He had been working in some sort of large Japanese corporation sitting in a small cubicle doing small tasks on a small computer. The company expanded but somehow did not have room for Yoshi's particular brand of smallness and he lost his job.

Yoshi has a wife and a small son and couldn't face telling them he had lost his job so he went home that day as if nothing had happened, thinking, "I'll tell them tomorrow". Then he got up the next day, put on his suit and took the train to Tokyo.

He's been doing this for over a year now, every day he kisses his wife and child goodbye, leaves for work and comes and sits on a bench eating his sushi and watching the world go by. I'm the first person, the very first person in over 400 days, to sit down next to him and offer the olive branch of polite conversation.

I like Yoshi, he's small, polite, well dressed and he looks like I might in a few years time if I were smaller, more polite, dressed smartly and had a sudden genetic leaning towards the previously unknown Japanese side of my family.

So I agreed to meet him here on his bench at the same time tomorrow.

WEEK 29 DAY 6

Before I meet Yoshi today I'm arranging a few things for him.

I've contacted his former employer in the Shiraishi business complex and found out where his old office was. I've arranged to lease a slightly larger office next to his old workplace, one where all his previous employers have to walk past to get to their office. I've bought him a big desk, a big computer and a big brass sign for his door. I hope he likes it.

I just left Yoshi in his new job, I've paid off his debts, I've arranged for a regular salary and I've given him, I hope, a new lease of life. I obviously made him promise he and his family will move to Shropshire when he retires, but that's decades away yet.

The only things he did have reservations about were the brass plaque saying "Japan's Ambassador to Shropshire" on his door and the life-size portrait of Carol Voderman I had hung behind his desk, but hey, I'm the boss. He really liked his big desk.

WEEK 29 DAY 7

Walking around Tokyo today, people seem worried about earthquakes, there's supposed to be a big one coming and they had this massive exercise recently where they practiced what they would do in case of a major tremor, it was sort of like a fire drill, but taken seriously.

I spent some time with a man called Kuroda feeding the birds with a plastic bag of breadcrumbs, who proudly told me that he could predict earthquakes.

He said that whenever a really serious quake is about to happen he feels it in his left leg. Then he rolled up his trousers and his leg looked like Noddy Holders top hat, all down his left leg he had drawing pins stuck into him, not the steel ones that maintain sterility in the packaging either but the cheaper brass ones used for notice boards and posters.

Kuroda told me the pins sing to him as a warning, then just as he was telling me he started humming in a sort of high pitched whine and shouted "It's coming! It's coming!" and made me hide under a bus shelter. After about half an hour he admitted that the drawing pins were not one hundred percent reliable and it was possibly a false alarm.

He was a very pleasant man though and we had a nice chat about Market Drayton and how there are hardly any earthquakes there. He said he really wanted to go live in Shropshire, but if there were no earthquakes there he would be wasting his gift and all those years sticking drawing pins in his leg would have been wasted.

It was hard to argue with him on that point so I left him, his leg shining in the Tokyo sunlight like a little disco for the birds.

WEEK 30 DAY 1

I was talking to a group of elderly people in downtown Tokyo today. They were worried that Japan is struggling to support it's rapidly ageing population.

According to a newspaper one of them showed me, the Japanese have the longest life expectancy in the world. It's attributed to their diet of mainly fish and vegetables; apparently 17,394 people in Japan are over the age of 100.

Apparently there has been a sharp rise in "grey on grey " crime recently here in Japan. That is, elderly people robbing other elderly people. I read a news article where a knife-wielding octogenarian man robbed an 84-year-old lady by breaking into her home via her bathroom window and saying "I am 80. Give me your money".

This sort of thing happened in Moreton Say once. A wiry, white-haired burglar was seen escaping from windows - leaping from roofs, and fleeing from crime scenes over a period of three months in the summer of 1992.

Only rare antique items of value were taken, no damage was done and no one heard the intruder until it was too late. One old lady who had her diamond-encrusted Peruvian eggcups stolen was quoted in the local paper as saying "He was in and out like a digestive in a cup of tea".

It was shortly after the crime wave that the "Twilight Hours" Retirement Home in Marchamley Wood got their new conservatory, sixty seater cinema, swimming pool and solarium installed. Nothing was ever proved but they have an inscribed breezeblock saying "Donated by Ronnie 'The Drainpipe' Thomas 1992" on the new buildings.

It doesn't take a mathematician to add the cinema, the conservatory, the pool and multiply it by the solarium to come up with Ronnie the Drainpipe. The gentleman thief was famous for once stealing the Seven Jeweled Star of Oswestry, Shropshire's answer to the Pink Panther.

The 93-year-old Ronnie could sometimes be seen in Market Drayton driving his golden mobility scooter, with his eye-patch, his wooden hand and a young nurse perched on the back. It always struck me as an excellent way to spend your final years.

I told the group of elderly people all about 'The Drainpipe'. They didn't seem to see the correlation between their situation and my story, there's just no helping some people .

WEEK 30 DAY 2

I've been thinking about all the old people in Japan. There are so many of them and they have so much free time. They seem like an ideal target audience.

I'm hiring a conference hall to do an "Introduction to Shropshire for Old People" talk. I've got a suitcase full of Yen and I'm going to make lots of old people very happy by offering them what every elderly Japanese person really wants, I'm going to offer them a happy retirement in Shropshire. The hall is booked for tomorrow.

Still lots to see in Tokyo. There are a surprising number of golden arches here, the big yellow M. I suppose it might be that the only culinary alternative is cold fish, but fast food seems incredibly popular.

The places are always stuffed full of burger devouring, milkshake sucking, fry spilling lost souls. Even the staff here seem happy, which can only be a result of the peculiar brand of brainwashing employed on fast food service employees.

For purely research purposes, I tried a burger, some fries and a thick chocolate shake. It was quite uncanny, they tasted exactly the same as they did when I last had a meal like this, the texture, the consistency, the flavour, the look, they were all exactly as they had been in Birmingham many months ago.

Terrible!

WEEK 30 DAY 3

For some reason, I've not been able to work out why people in Japan give each other melons as gifts.

You can buy them with little bows tied around them and a message tag so your special gift melon can be personalised.

Now I can understand buying someone a nice little pottery cottage, or a new bingo marker, or a calendar, or a snowstorm, or a novelty rubber, or one of those lovely personalised key rings with the meaning of your name on, or a regionally appropriate fridge magnet; but a large, round fruit is the last thing I'd expect as a pressie.

Anyway, I turned up at the conference hall with a van full of melons as a gift to all the old people before they sat through my 4-hour "Introduction to Shropshire for Old People" talk that I spent all last night preparing.

I'd bought some stationary early this morning to add an air of professionalism to the proceedings. I had a flip chart, a pointer, four different colours of marker, props and everything.

Before I'd even finished unloading the melons, a group of quite burly old people rushed me. I'm not saying "a group" when there were only one or two, there really was a large hunting pack of OAPs.

I'm not saying "burly" when really they had Zimmer frames, arthritis and an average weight of 6 stone. These were beefed up, muscular old people, probably on steroids or something.

I'm not saying "rushed me" out of some retrospective attempt to save face and exaggerate the speed of the assault; they really did leap from nowhere like a swarm of angry bees. Angry, elderly, burly bees.

They stole all my yen, they stole my van and to add insult to injury, a particularly large old person took one of the melons between his hands, twisted it into two halves and threw it to the ground. He shouted something at me in Japanese and hopped into the back of the van as it sped away.

I was most upset.

After that, I went into the conference hall that I had so lovingly prepared. Three little old ladies were sat waiting at the front. Behind them were several hundred empty seats.

I was quite prepared to give my talk without the aid of flip-charts, pointers, markers or melons, but the three remaining old people were apparently just waiting for a game of Bingo that was due to start in the adjoining hall.

When I asked if I could join in with the Bingo, they told me I had to be a member. I asked how I could join and they said that I was quite welcome to join then and there, but that I had to be over 60, Japanese and pay the entrance fee. I told them I'd think about it and walked back to the hotel.

Today was not one of my most successful days .

WEEK 30 DAY 4

Sat in my hotel room all morning and looked out the window.

Feeling a bit deflated about yesterday.

This afternoon I reported the van to the hire company and went to the bank to fill another suitcase full of Yen.

I'm not going to let one isolated incident stop my resolve. People need to know about Shropshire, and who else is there to tell the people of Japan?

You might think it's unwise of me to keep filling suitcases full of Japanese currency and walking around with them, but I believe in the basic goodness of all people and I intend to use this money to promote Shropshire. Who would want to steal from such a worthy cause?

I'm sure yesterdays melon-jacking was an isolated incident.

WEEK 30 DAY 5

Tried to see if they had the Shropshire-based classic 'Gone To Earth' on the hotel pay-per-view film catalogue.

They didn't.

They just had lots of Japanese films. Most of them seem to include monsters (generally giant reptiles) or schoolgirls or in one case schoolgirls that mutated into giant reptiles.

I've arranged to give a slightly lower key talk today to a group of elderly Japanese people just outside Tokyo in a place called Kumagaya. I'm not going to be giving melons this time.

I'm standing in the porch of the building that is supposed to be hosting my talk on "An Introduction to Shropshire for Old People". No one is answering the door.

This is terrible. I was just typing that last entry on my palmtop when an old lady, possibly eighty or ninety, she looked a bit like an older Dewi Sukarno, pushed past me, grabbed my case full of yen and locked the outer door. She jumped in a van that looked suspiciously like the one I hired a few days ago and left at speed.

I'm stuck in the porch now. No one seems to be around. It's quite cold.

I just rang my Mother, I haven't heard from her for a while. Apparently she had been down in London with Toby, Sophia and Aunt Felicity to see David Blaine.

She's never been to London before so they stayed on for a few days. She says that Sophia is now visibly pregnant and her and Toby are doing really well. meanwhile, Aunt Felicity got thrown out of Madame Tussauds for trying to pull the head off David Jason.

Mother told me they were there when David Blaine was released. Apparently he'd been sealed in a plastic box for 44 days and survived on only water. When he was released he said it was a life changing experience and it helped him appreciate the simple things.

I told Mother I was trapped in a Japanese porch; she didn't believe me.

I've been in this porch for three hours now. An old man walked past about an hour ago, he said something to me in Japanese and walked away. He didn't come back. I'm settling down to sleep the night here now, I'm sure someone will come along in the morning .

WEEK 30 DAY 6

It's morning. I'm still trapped in the porch. I tried to break the glass, but I just bounced off it. It must be some sort of safety, anti-theft glass or something.

It was a cold night, the letterbox let in a terrible draft.

It's noon now, the sun is high in the sky. I managed to attract the attention of a young man that was walking past by shouting through the letterbox, he came over and talked to me for a while, but his English was about as good as my Japanese.

The young man returned about an hour later with a few of his friends and they are sat on a wall watching me now.

A few more people have gathered. I'm trying to get the message across to them that I'm thirsty and hungry and trapped, but none of my mimes seem to get the message across. I tried to express through the medium of charade that I needed someone to unlock the door, but they just applauded.

I notice some of them have brought flasks and sandwiches. They are eating them only a few feet away from the porch. It's very annoying.

David Blaine at least had a constant supply of water, all I've had since yesterday are the few drops of rainwater I managed to drink by putting my tongue through the letterbox. I'm not doing that again, it's one of those letterboxes with the brown brush fixture in the opening, it's fine on the way out, but it really hurts your tongue when you pull it back.

It's getting dark now and I'm weak from thirst and hunger. I took off my shoe and starting banging it on the glass of the porch. The crowd seemed to like this and started to sing some Japanese songs to the beat of my shoe, so I stopped. Unfortunately they kept on singing anyway.

I've noticed from watching Japanese television that the culture seems to encourage suffering as a form of entertainment. Perhaps they think that I'm part of some sort of game show.

Most of the onlookers have dispersed now, only two hardcore watchers are staying. They have brought a little tent and a stove. None came near enough today for me to grab them, no one tried to open the porch or give me any food or water.

I'm tired now and I'm going to try and sleep.

WEEK 30 DAY 7

In the night some people started poking sticks through the letterbox. They prodded me awake and then ran off. I hate it when people do things like that.

At 8.00am this morning an old man came with a big set of keys and opened the porch, he shouted something at me (I really wish people here would make more of an effort to learn a little elementary English), and pushed me out of the porch. I was glad to leave.

The couple in the tent waved, cheered and clapped as I left for my hotel. I gave them my notes from the "Introduction to Shropshire for Old People" talk. I don't feel the time or the place is right for giving that particular lecture.

Despite recent events, I still believe in the inherent goodness present in most people. When you get down to it, people only do bad things because they feel they have to. They do good things because they want to.

No matter how terrible a person's crimes may be, how abhorrent their personality, how devoid of moral fibre they might appear to be, if you appeal to their better nature and give them an opportunity to do the right thing, then redemption is always possible.

117

With this in mind I intend to continue my journey unsullied by past unpleasantness.

I will strive to spread the creamy paste of Shropshire goodness on the sliced loaf of humanity and see if anyone bites.

Everyone, everywhere, whoever they are, deserves to know about the joys of Salopian living and has within them a potential citizen of Shropshire.

With the exceptions, of course, being Camilla Edwards and whoever decided to change Countdown's broadcast time to 3.15 p.m.

WEEK 31 DAY 1

I used to work with a lady called Eunice who resembled a young Bette Midler and would only eat things that began with the first 13 letters of the alphabet. Anything after 'M' was in her eyes, inedible and disgusting.

She was oddly obsessive about it, but never really thought it through and had her own special rules for what was and was not acceptable.

For example, she used to have chips for lunch (without the salt or vinegar of course) until someone pointed out that they were made from potatoes, so instead she starting bringing in bread and cheese. She would never put the cheese inside the bread, because then it would be a sandwich.

She was quite happy to have a Tupperware container full of apple, bread, cheese, and coleslaw. Quite happy, that is, until someone else pointed out that apple, bread, cheese, and coleslaw was practically a ploughman's lunch and therefore beyond the boundary of "M".

I think people kept finding fault in her eating logic in a well-meaning attempt to break the cycle and stop her compulsive behaviour, but it wasn't long before she realised that all vegetables were over the alphabetical limit and she went off sick with scurvy and we didn't hear of her again.

The reason I bring this up is that I met Kuroda again today and he was sitting on a bench eating some bread and cheese from a Tupperware container. Kuroda is a small Japanese man with a pleasant, friendly manner and a leg full of drawing pins.

He claims to use these pins to predict earthquakes - they sing to him as a special warning that only he can hear.

After a previous false alarm, I was sceptical as to the accuracy of his predictions. So when he started the high-pitched humming again and insisted I climb into a large metal refuse container I was initially hesitant. I do think it's important to show you believe in people, no matter how odd they may seem, or how sceptical you may actually be.

I hopped into the container full of damp cardboard as both an act of solidarity and a way to prove to myself that people often need to be trusted before they can trust you.

As it turned out, I was glad I did jump in with Kuroda. After less than a minute sat next to him, among the out-of-date sushi, Tokyo suffered it's biggest quake for ages.

Kuroda and myself were shaken around in the metal bin like a refuse cocktail as it rained roof tiles and the ground split open.

Kuroda shrugged off my profuse thanks and swaggered off down the broken road with that air of smug self-satisfaction you get when you've spent the last few years living on the edge of society and then finally you predict an earthquake with pinpoint accuracy.

WEEK 31 DAY 2

There's been a lot on the news about an unmanned mission to mars getting cancelled. I've been watching a lot of news on my hotel television, and it never ceases to amaze me how blinkered and biased the world-view of the media is.

The channel I was watching devoted a full twenty minutes to the story about the mars mission and not once did they mention Shropshire's manned flight to Mars in 1978.

In fact noteworthy things happen all the time that never make the news.

You can't buy a paper without a lengthy article giving the minutiae of some celebrity's love life; but you rarely (if ever) hear of Samuel Longhorn, the famous eighties womaniser of Skyborry Green, who fathered 817 children between 1987 and 1999.

He wrote extensive diaries that were only ever serialised in the Skyborry Green Reporter, a photocopied local publication with a circulation of 72.

You hear all about the royal butler writing a book; but no one mentions the Windsor-Gibbons family who live in a mobile home just outside Babbinswood. They are an offshoot of the Royal family, disowned during Queen Victoria's reign and all mention of them removed from official record.

But if you buy a toasted teacake at the truckers' sandwich van on the road into Babbinswood, chances are that it's a princess that gives you your change. You can't miss it, it's the van with the fried egg painted on the side, and dead centre of the yolk is a royal crest.

Yes, you only hear what they want you to hear.

Which is why I must soldier on and tell people of a place where wonders happen that they could only dream about (and then only if they ate particularly indigestible cheese shortly before bedtime)... A place where the sunlight is brighter, the grass is greener, the sandwiches are nicer and everyone is terribly pleasant to each other, especially Samuel Longhorn... a place called Shropshire.

WEEK 31 DAY 3

I'm a bit bored today.

Not having much luck in getting Japan on my side.

I tried dressing up as a gingerbread man and going to a Japanese bakery convention to tell them about Market Drayton and it's superior cakes and pastries, but security wouldn't let me in.

After trying several different ways to enter the venue, a particularly large security guard threatened to bite my head off and pulled off one of my eyes; so I gave in.

Not before I sellotaped the recipe for a particularly succulent gingerbread to the fire exit though - that'll show them!

WEEK 31 DAY 4

The people in Japan always seem to be concentrating on something.

If you sit on a bench and watch the populous pass you by, they all have that pondering expression, that betrayal of internal activity that your face displays when you are trying to retrieve a bit of information you know you know, but can't quite put your finger on the right synapse.

In a bid to understand this apparent preoccupation, I tried stopping a few people and asking them "What are you thinking about?". The first six either didn't understand me or chose not to; but the seventh person I stopped looked me square in the eye and said "Shropshire".

Aha I thought. At last, my suspicions are confirmed, the spirit of Shropshire lies dormant in every culture. If you catch them at the right moment, the motherland is actually never that far away from anyone's mind.

As it turned out, the person I stopped was called Terrance Smith and was on his way to the airport, about to return to the gleaming spires of Telford and his bedsit on Victoria Road.

WEEK 31 DAY 5

I followed a man from Shropshire to the airport yesterday and on an impulse I got a last minute seat on a flight to Alaska.

On reflection this might not have been such a wise move, partly because I don't really know much about Alaska; partly because there is still much to do to convince the people of Japan to adopt a more Salopian mindset... but mostly because my luggage is still at the hotel in Tokyo.

I'm on the plane now. It's a long flight and we stop off at a few places on the way. They won't let me get off the plane though, so I just have to sit here and look out the window. It's a bit like being back at my old job in the office, sitting here knowing I can't go anywhere yet; except at the office I could at least make little men out of paperclips.

Paperclips have a myriad of interesting uses. In fact I read somewhere (it might have been the West Country Office Consumables Monthly) that only 1 in 10 paperclips is ever actually used for clipping paper.

The other 90 percent get up to all sorts of fascinating things - they are useful as toothpicks, tiny coat-hangers, fuses, stress relievers *(either by flicking them across the office or bending them into interesting shapes), hooks; you can spend hours making them into chains like some high-tech modern, metal equivalent to the daisy and you can bend them into small purpose-built tools for all manner of jobs from unblocking staplers to indelibly etching your name on the photocopier.

I love paperclips. I wish I had some on me now. I asked the flight attendant if she had any but all she could offer were peanuts or a hot towel.

WEEK 31 DAY 6

Still on the plane.

We had some delays due to bad weather. The plane had to stay on the runway of an airport somewhere between Japan and Alaska. It was very white outside, like the plane had landed in a glass of milk.

There isn't much in the way of literature on the plane that might tell me about what to expect in Alaska, so I ended up watching something on the plane about Britney Spears.

There was this musical video with Madonna where Britney seemed to be wearing more than one pair of braces and kept taking them on and off.

It baffled me - braces are a perfectly reasonable way for a gentleman to keep his trousers up and a viable alternative to the belt or elasticated waist. But why would a teenage pop princess need more than one pair, and why did she keep taking them off and on and crossing them back and forth over her shoulders?

I composed a brief letter to Ms Spears' management, suggesting she buy a belt and while she was at it, concentrate less on the collaborations with music industry legends and more on the sort of folk music so popular in Shropshire during the 1970s.

WEEK 31 DAY 7

I'm in Alaska.

It's cold, and dark, and the people all seem quite large. It reminds me a bit of Ludlow in November.

I'm staying at a boarding house run by an old lady called Miriam who looks like a really, really old waxwork model of Queen Victoria, only sporting a luxuriant ginger moustache.

Miriam has given me the attic room; the only rule she stipulates is that I must not under any circumstances open the window in my room. I asked her why not and she said "Isn't it obvious?"

Having spent four hours sitting on my bed looking at the window, I still have no idea why I can't open it. It looks like quite a new window and the handle looks normal, except for the little sticker above the catch that says, "Do not open this window".

I didn't open the window.

Maybe tomorrow.

WEEK 32 DAY 1

It looks like it's going to be a white Christmas for me this year, which I suppose is to be expected when you consider that I'm not in Moreton Say anymore, I'm in Anchorage, Alaska.

I flew in via Anchorage international airport yesterday, ready to take on what the brochure calls "the last frontier" - which coincidentally is what my Mother used to call Telford Town Park.

I do feel a bit like a pioneer in the Wild West, ready to take my exciting new ideas to a world unfamiliar with such delights; forge a new path through an untamed land, except without all the bloodshed and genocide associated with the founding fathers of America.

I'm staying in the attic room of a boarding house and looking out of the closed window at the falling snow. I mentioned, not complained, just mentioned, to the landlady Miriam that I was a little bit cold last night.

She said "What do you expect? Central heating?"

I said "Well, yes…"

She said "You haven't opened that window have you?" and then walked off.

That's about the sum total of my conversations in Alaska so far. Maybe it's just the cultural differences that I need to overcome, but I get the distinct feeling Miriam doesn't like me very much. It's not just the heating thing, I paid for bed and breakfast, but when I woke up this morning there was a note under the door that said:

Breakfast menu –

Toast.

Unfortunately the following items are not available for breakfast this morning-

Toast

NB Please do not open the window

I tried to open the window, it wouldn't move.

WEEK 32 DAY 2

Today I tried to interest the local Anchorage press in my worldwide quest to promote all things Shropshire.

I went round all the press offices I could find. I spoke to editors, advertisers, publishers, columnists, photographers, receptionists and reporters... but mostly to receptionists.

No one took me up on my offer of an in-depth feature article on me, but I did manage to put a few classified ads in next week's papers.

"Unhappy? Cold? Don't worry, just move to Shropshire and all your troubles will be over. For more info contact M. Telford at...." And I gave the address of Miriam's guesthouse. I hope she doesn't mind.

I've tried to get the world's media on my side before, and I'd be the first to admit that I have had only limited success. However, I'm optimistic that my new more personal approach will work wonders.

WEEK 32 DAY 3

I met a man called Jimmy today.

The locals call him 'Jimmy the Flake', who's from Shropshire's slightly backward cousin, Devon.

Jimmy told me he was in Alaska because of a drunken bet he made on New Year's Eve 1999.

It turns out that he was with some friends in a Cowboy themed bar, drinking cocktails with names like Bucking Bronco and High Noon. He was much the worse-for-wear and heralding in the New Year.

Jimmy got into an argument about the unique nature of the snowflake - He postulated that there were only a finite number of physical forms the humble snowflake could adopt; and that given enough time and enough snow, he could easily find a few naturally occurring duplicates - Thus disproving what his mate Harry had said in the bar, that each snowflake is unique.

Before he had sobered up properly, he was on the first flight to Anchorage. Since then, Jimmy's bought a large freezer, a microscope, a nice solid shovel and begun his challenge in earnest.

Four years and several million snowflakes later, Jimmy now has a complex state-of-the-art computer-imaging library and is the northern hemisphere's premiere authority on snowflake formations.

He still hasn't found two the same though.

Jimmy admitted to me that he is now sick of the sight of snow, and dreams of the day he finds twin flakes. However, he refuses to give up looking; or cheat and pretend he's found one - and I admire that.

While the original bet was only for a tenner, Jimmy reckons he has now spent in the region of £184,000 on the project.

I suggested to him that he take a break from it all, have a few weeks in Shropshire, but he was too worried that he might miss the elusive duo he is searching for; that if he takes his eyes off the snowfall for too long, a pair of snowflake clones will sneak by without him knowing.

It was hard to argue with him, but I tried for a bit anyway, then went back to Miriam and the window.

WEEK 32 DAY 4

I went to one of the main streets of Anchorage today with a large "Visit Shropshire, it's much warmer there" sign. After a while it occurred to me that being warmer than Alaska wasn't such a bold claim, and changed the sign to the more direct "Visit Shropshire, it's much better there."

Unfortunately some aggressive locals (One of them dressed as Santa) couldn't handle the bare truth displayed so overtly - they took offence and forcibly removed my sign and me.

I was a bit bruised and went back to the guesthouse early, but Miriam was out and she has the only key.

I noticed a ladder in her back garden so I tried some of the upper floor windows - none of them would open.

I sat on the cold doorstep and sat in a big, slightly frozen over pool of self-pity until she arrived home.

WEEK 32 DAY 5

While wandering throughout Anchorage today (Trying to promote all things Salopian), I got talking to a young man called Pedro who was seated at the roadside with an easel, painting furiously.

Pedro (Who I noticed looked not unlike a young Salvador Dali, but with an afro) was an artist who specialised in painting doorways. He works his way up the streets of Anchorage, painting, drawing, and sometimes sculpturing, the doorways of the houses, buildings, shops and garages.

I asked him what fascinates him so much about doors.

He told me that a doorway is a new beginning; a portal to fresh possibilities and the most exciting thing on this earth.

I told him that if he thinks doorways are the most exciting thing on earth, then he should try gingerbread, or go and see Ironbridge. Bridges are better than doors; you can see what you are getting into.

It's very, very cold so I went back to my room early and tried to open the window by slotting spoons into the frame and prising the window open in much the same way you might remove a tyre from a bicycle.

It didn't work.

WEEK 32 DAY 6

I rang Mother, with it being Christmas I thought she might have called me, but there was no answer. Christmas is always a special time at the Telford home, I learned quite early on in my life that Father Christmas is a fabrication, so you can imagine how glad I was when Mother told me all about Old Mother Shropshire and her magic badger who spins magic threads across the continents every December giving special gifts to Salopians all over the world. I used to sit on Mother's knee and point out in the Argos catalogue what I would like most and as if by magic, Old Mother Shropshire would know what I wanted and put some of my smaller and less expensive choices in the stocking I had left by my bed. I feel I've been an extra good boy this year so I fully expect an extra special present. I've left my stocking up in my room at Miriam's boarding house for Old Mother Shropshire to fill with exciting things. I don't have access to any of the customary gingerbread or port to leave for the festive gift giver, but I did leave a note explaining why they were absent and a packet of mints as compensation.

WEEK 32 DAY 7

I woke up this morning, rushed to my stocking to see what Old Mother Shropshire had brought me.

Nothing.

Not a thing.

I bet it's that window. Old Mother Shropshire probably came all the way to Alaska and was thwarted by a hermetically sealed window.

It's the last straw! I've checked myself out of the boarding house, but not before getting a crowbar to the window in my room.

It opened about half an inch and then the ceiling collapsed! The window seemed to be all that was holding up that part of the roof. Miriam really should have warned me not to open the window.

I rang Mother again.

Still no answer.

I expect she is too upset that I am not there with her over Christmas and has gone for a walk to cheer herself up.

Not one person has replied to my advert in the papers, so I've hired a sled and some dogs. I'm going to greet the New Year in the frozen wastes and try to find someone, maybe an Eskimo, who really needs to know all about Shropshire.

Anchorage is sort of at the middle bottom of Alaska. I'm going to travel north into the interior, past Fairbanks and up into the northern tip at Prudhoe Bay.

Some people might think it unwise to set out alone like this into the frozen tundra, especially without any sort of training as to how you drive a pack of Huskies. But I'm confident that I'll pick it up as I go along.

I've got a shoe full of local currency, eight packets of mints, a thermal vest, some paperclips and a Shropshire born fire in my heart!

How can 2004 not be the official Year of Morris?

WEEK 33 DAY 1

No more houses, no more doors, and most especially no more windows... just me, my pack of loyal huskies and the frozen tundra.

Nut much in the way of townss or vilagges, just lots of snoow and twrees, the dogs pretty much steer themselvves which is just as wellk since holdin on takes most of my energyyy. It's hard typing on my palmtop whirle im wearing thesbe enorbous glubves.

WEEK 33 DAY 2

I've found another use for paperclips. I've bent them into small spirals with a prong pointing from the middle. I've fixed them on the end of my gloved fingers, that way I can still type on my palmtop while I wear gloves.

Paperclips truly are the universal tool, the stationary equivalent of the Swiss army knife - capable of any task.

I'm becoming quite attached to the pack of huskies that are pulling me across Alaska. I was told the names of the dogs when I hired them, but after a day I've forgotten them all, so I've renamed them after famous Salopians.

Clive of India had a bit of a fight with Christopher Timothy earlier and I had to separate them with a tree branch. Thomas Telford urinated on Percy Thrower. Percy retaliated by trying to mount him and Sandy Lyle MBE ate all my mints.

I've been trying to head north and should have come across a township by now. However, all I've come across for the last couple of days is snow, ice, trees and what I think was a life-size replica of Much Wenlock Library encased in ice, but I was very cold and tired when I saw that and it might just have been a hill.

Mostly its just snow.

The Huskies seemed to know where they were going, so I pretty much left them to it. I think that I may have overestimated their canine navigation skills.

I think I might be lost.

WEEK 33 DAY 3

I'm trying to keep warm at night by sleeping between Percy Thrower and Clive of India. This worked out fine until I woke up this morning all tangled up in harnesses and straps.

I cut myself free by sawing at the straps with the ends of paperclips... but this allowed all but one of the dogs to run off.

The dogs were still strapped together, so perhaps they think I'm still being towed behind them. They might come back when they notice I'm missing. I hope I'm not expecting too much of them.

I'm going to wait.

I'm still waiting.

I don't think they are coming back.

I'm stuck now in the middle of Alaska, in freezing temperatures, with only a sled and Sandy Lyle MBE for company. I'm not sure even the paperclips will help me get out of this.

WEEK 33 DAY 4

I think it's New Years day today, though the calendar on my palmtop PC says 01/14/99. I don't think it was designed to operate in these sub-zero Alaskan temperatures.

Actually, neither was I. I'm afraid I might have frostbite. My ears are incredibly cold; I think a bit of my right ear snapped off last night, but I might just have dreamt it.

I let Sandy Lyle MBE go in the early hours. I'm sleepy with the cold and that made me think of my Star Wars duvet cover at home in Moreton Say.

I started looking at Sandy and thinking of the start of The Empire Strikes Back where Luke Skywalker keeps warm by cutting open his Tauntaun. Then I started trying to make a light sabre out of paperclips, but fortunately I came to my senses and thought I'd better let the dog go before I get any more Jedi delusions.

He was whining and uneasy anyway and I thought he probably stood a better chance on his own. I cut him free and he shot off into the white night like a number four iron drive with a headwind.

I hope he finds his own doggy equivalent of Shropshire.

Just before dawn I saw a light in the distance and left my sled behind to stumble towards it. I thought it might be a passing snowmobile, or a small building, or just a fire surrounded by burly but friendly Alaskans with hot tasty snacks and a hospitable nature.

After about an hour I realised it was just the sun rising. That was a bit of a disappointment. I've lost my sled now too.

I've fashioned a rudimentary pair of skis from tree branches and paperclips and I'm trying to make as much ground as I can before darkness, starvation, frostbite and loneliness set in.

WEEK 33 DAY 5

Just before dark last night the photocopier of fate successfully performed a duplex A3 collated copy in my favour and I found civilisation once again.

I came across a rough track and followed it to a crudely painted sign that welcomed me to,

"Lost Hope, Alaska, population -34"

It's a lovely little place, a bit like Ellesmere but without the pub restaurant or ducks.

I don't like the name though. You can lose your money, your self-respect, your mind, your signed photograph of Carol Vorderman, your hearing, your hair or your favourite bingo marker; but hope is the one thing you must never lose.

I've misplaced mine a couple of times, but it's always turned up. The secret is to think of the last place you had it.

The population is stated as minus 34 on the sign. Apparently they have had more deaths than births now for 137 consecutive years.

Each time someone dies they deduct one from the number on the sign, each time someone is born they add one. Somewhere along the line they lost count.

When I arrived I walked into a bar and they were very welcoming. A lovely man called Roland, who is wider than he is tall, told me, as he wrapped me in warm towels, that I'd never, ever want to leave.

He obviously doesn't know yet that I am on an important mission. I'll tell him later when I get the feeling back in my legs and head.

WEEK 33 DAY 6

...

WEEK 33 DAY 7

I slept all yesterday. At least I think I did, or it might be the calendar on my Palmtop not working properly again. It still seems to be sending this to the BBC... I hope someone is reading this.

I'm starting 2004 in a little Alaskan town called "Lost Hope". I'm staying in a room above the local bar; it's quite cosy, especially compared to the divan of frozen ice I have been sleeping on.

Over the last few days I have once again hung precariously over the deep fat fryer of death, only to be left uncooked at the very last moment.

I feel quite unstoppable again now, filled to the very brim with enthusiasm. I'm committed to telling the poor frozen souls of Lost Hope that there is indeed hope left alive in the world... approximately four and a half thousand miles away, just off the M6, in the warm and welcoming bosom of Shropshire.

I rang Mother again just now, still no answer. I hope she is alright. It's not like her to leave the house for more than a few hours; she worries about the cows breaking into the kitchen and drinking from the sink.

I'll try her again tomorrow.

The locals all seem to come to the bar at night, so I'm going to go down tonight and thank them all for helping me out... Then I'll explain to them that they should all move to Shropshire.

They seem like a perfectly nice bunch of people - all beards, muscles and red check shirts. I'm sure I'll fit right in.

I thought I might convince them to have a Bingo night in the bar this week as well. They don't know how lucky they are that I have stumbled into their lives, but they soon will.

WEEK 34 DAY 1

I gave a brief but eventful presentation to a packed bar last night.

Setting up, it reminded me of the halcyon days in my old office job when I would give my weekly stationary report in the team meetings - Twenty five minutes on how many post it notes we had used since last Tuesday. I was often chastised for the length, depth and content of my presentations, but I like to think I added a flavour and colour to otherwise dull proceedings.

My presentation theme in the bar was, as always, why Shropshire is so completely marvelous in every single way and how it can solve all your problems with its aforementioned marvellousness.

I had barely set up a makeshift flipchart and begun describing the gentle beauty of Moreton Say before a group of men in white hoods burst in and put a bag over my head. I think it was a bag, but it all happened so suddenly it might have been just a piece of cloth wrapped around my face, like a large blindfold, or a small sack.

I was bundled into a vehicle of some sort and driven a small distance. Then the bag or possibly sack was removed and a light shone directly in my face in a fashion often seen in World War Two film interrogations... but seldom in real life.

I was sitting on a chair in the middle of a small wooden room. Men in white hoods were at the periphery of my vision, brandishing things menacingly in their hands, like bits of pipe and crowbars. However, I did notice a couple of them had spatulas and one of them had what looked very much like an egg whisk.

Anyway there was much shouting and pushing around, but nothing a hardened traveller such as myself couldn't handle.

The nature of the display seemed to be that I was not allowed to give talks in public places, or to promote any alternative lifestyles to the one currently on offer in Lost Hope, unless I had the express permission of the Pope.

After a bit of confusion I ascertained that this wasn't the Vatican-based Pope, but a locally based Pope, who seemed to be behind this reactionary little display.

I calmly explained that I'd like to meet the Pope. After a bit of forced laughing and bizarre Wizard of Oz type comments like "Nobody, but nobody sees the Pope", I managed to make an appointment for tomorrow and they re-bagged my head and led me out.

Despite all the pushing and lights and bags over heads, my abductors seemed like a decent enough bunch of people. I couldn't help but notice they stopped me banging my head as they put me back in the vehicle and put my seatbelt on for me before driving me back to the bar.

One of them even said "sorry" when I knocked my arm as he pushed me out of the car.

WEEK 34 DAY 2

I was taken to meet a man called "The Pope" today.

He lives in the largest house in Lost Hope - a mansion in the snow... All roman columns, Gone With The Wind staircases, stuffed animal heads, unspoken menace and high ceilings.

I was left to wait for a full half hour on a hard stone bench, with not so much as a cup of tea or digestive biscuit, before being summoned into his presence.

I was going to complain about the wait and lack of digestives, before then threatening to withhold vital information about Shropshire and the glories within...

However, when I saw that the Pope was wearing what appeared to be a garment of human skin, with an ermine trim and had a large snake coiled at his feet, I thought better of it.

He was clearly a man intent on giving the appearance of menace.

After a short chat with the Pope, in which I tried to explain to him the importance of Shropshire and he tried to explain to me that if I talk out of turn once again he would have me killed, I feel we came to a mutual understanding.

I want to tell the people of Lost Hope that the welcoming vistas of my beloved Shropshire are waiting for them just across the ocean... While the Pope wants me to understand that as patriarch of Lost Hope, I must obey his every whim and spend the rest of my natural life living in fear of displeasing him.

WEEK 34 DAY 3

I hid in my room above the bar all day today.

Outside on the telegraph pole someone has stuck a billposter saying "Don't talk to strangers, it's better for your health". It's actually quite good advice given the predatory nature of some individuals in today's society and something I would encourage all parents to tell their children.

In this context however, I think it's directed at me specifically.

I'm not leaping to conclusions here.

The poster was put up after the xenophobic past few days... It's been displayed just outside the window of my room... It's in red writing - a clear indication of threatful intent rather than friendly advice... and there's an artists impression of me on it.

It's not a bad likeness actually.

It's really quite upset me that elements of the Lost Hope community feel this way toward me.

I'm a stranger to no man; I'm Morris Telford, friend to the world.

WEEK 34 DAY 4

I left my room briefly today to see what all the noise outside was about.

There was a parade in the street outside and they seemed to be burning an effigy. I'm not leaping to conclusions here, but I think it was supposed to be me.

It was wearing the same clothes, had the same hair, the same build, again it's not a bad likeness actually... obviously someone in Lost Hope has real artistic talent.

However, the real giveaway was the sign around the neck saying "Morris Telford".

They certainly know how to give a bloke a welcome here.

WEEK 34 DAY 5

It's some sort of local tradition that on this day each year they take the newest member of the community and dip him headfirst into the freezing waters of Lake Hell, which in contradiction of the popular phrase, is nearly always frozen over.

They call it the "Day Of Death", I'm sure it's all in good fun.

I now know why Roland was so glad to see me the first day I arrived. He had been here six months and was due for a dipping himself as newest entrant to Lost Hope.

They are banging at my door now; they certainly are enthusiastic about local customs in Lost Hope. I hope I can channel some of this zeal into an appreciation of Shropshire.

I'd better go and answer it, before they break it down.

WEEK 34 DAY 6

I'm a bit down today.

Partly because I was nearly killed yesterday when I was dropped into a frozen lake and left for dead; partly because the people here seem to have it in for me; but mostly because I've had some bad news on the phone.

I rang home and when I finally managed to get a signal, Aunt Felicity answered and told me the terrible, terrible news.

My Mother has died.

She was on the roof trying to fix the guttering. They have had a lot of snow in Moreton Say this week and as it was melting on the roof it was running down into the corner of my old bedroom.

Since Toby moved out Mother had arranged everything exactly as it had been when I had left - My mounted collection of rare Bingo markers from around the world, my magazine clippings of Richard Whiteley, my Star Wars duvet and the drawing of Clive Of India I did in HB Pencil.

She didn't want the rain to spoil my room for when I came home, so she was outside in high winds trying to sellotape the guttering back into place.

I've told her a thousand times that sellotape (while a revolutionary repair tool in the case of most paper or cardboard based situations), is not an industrial strength bonding tape and should not be used for electrical insulation, plumbing or muzzling dogs.

She always had misplaced enthusiasm for sellotape's ability to mend anything and it was, quite literally, her downfall.

She fell, plucked from the roof by gale force winds and landed on the greenhouse. Her fall was broken by a rusty Mini engine and lots of glass.

She didn't stand a chance and I feel at least partly responsible.

WEEK 34 DAY 7

I went to see the Pope again, explained the situation and asked if I could please leave Lost Hope and go home for my Mother's funeral.

He said No.

He said lots of other things, but the theme of the thing was definitely "No".

I don't like the Pope.

On the way back to my single room I cried like I haven't cried since I left my beloved Moreton Say, 34 weeks ago.

My tears froze on my reddened cheeks, little, salty jewels of pure sorrow preserved beyond their time.

I want my Mum.

WEEK 35 DAY 1

I can't stay here.

I want to go home.

I feel victimised, vilified and very alone. It's like working in the reprographics room all over again, but this time I can't go and hide in the stationary cupboard until it's time to go home.

Why are they so keen on keeping me here?

The only thing I have to offer them, my knowledge of Shropshire and it's wonderful ways, I'm not permitted to talk about.

It's not like I'm some fanatical weirdo misfit trying to force myself upon them. I'm just an enthusiastic, misplaced traveller offering an interesting new point of view.

I walked to the edge of town today and tried to keep going into the icy wilderness beyond. The Pope sent his men after me and I was hauled back again before I was out of sight.

When I did get back, a man called Greg, who looked like an overweight Anthony Newley, made me a hot chocolate and was quite sympathetic. He even put little multi-coloured marshmallows in my drink, so maybe some of the people here haven't lost all hope after all.

Greg has been here for three years now. I asked him why he doesn't leave, he said, "I tried" and held up his left hand as evidence. Bits of it were missing.

WEEK 35 DAY 2

I demanded to see the Pope again today. I was led into a waiting room again and told to wait.

It was a funny little room that smelled of sweet decay and it had stuffed animal heads on the walls - but they were all really sad little animals, like a stuffed beaver head, a chipmunk, an arctic fox, what I think was just a ginger tom but the label said lynx, and a rather sorry looking lemming.

I half expected there to be an empty mount at the end of the room with a little label on the bottom of it that said "Morris".

All the little heads stared at me with their dead, glassy eyes, except the lemming that seemed to be looking wistfully at the ceiling.

I've always quite liked lemmings. People tend to associate them with mass suicide, a sort of hamster branch of the Heaven's Gaters, but the truth is, lemmings never jump off cliffs en masse, at least not of their own volition.

As with so many things in life, Walt Disney is to blame. In 1958 Disney were making a documentary called "White Wilderness" and deliberately herded a whole bunch of lemmings straight off a cliff, filmed it and the myth was born. Terrible business, really.
In reality, the only flightless mammals foolish enough to deliberately hurl themselves off cliffs have two legs, less hair and an unending predisposition for stupidity.

I waited for nearly an hour and then gave up and tried to use the door. It was locked.

When I tried to turn the handle I could hear giggling from the other side of the door.

This is a classic bullying situation and they should think themselves lucky I'm not in a workplace situation, or I would report them to the local harassment officer and there would be serious repercussions.

It was another two hours before they unlocked the door and a very large man (who looked like he had never smiled) told me the Pope was too busy to see me now and that I should come back tomorrow.

I told the man my Mother had died and I just wanted to go home. He just said, "Everybody dies".

Fortunately, I know from experience that the best way to deal with bullies is to stand up to them. They are often the biggest cowards underneath all that aggression and muscle and anger.

So I poked my finger in the very large man's chest, intending to give him a severe telling off (with emphasis on taking into account other people's feelings in the way you behave), but I only got as far as the initial finger jab.

I'm sitting on the bare floorboards in my room above the bar now trying to type this with my thumbs... all my other fingers are broken.

WEEK 35 DAY 3

I may have exaggerated yesterday.

When I awoke this morning I could once again move my fingers, so it's unlikely they were broken. But they were certainly quite badly bruised and it will be some time before I play the honky-tonk again.

In the street outside they are hanging a mural from the roof of the building opposite. It's a giant picture of the Pope, sitting on a throne of ivory, smiling down at me, and holding a hand grenade in one hand and a baseball bat with a nail in it in the other... A bit like a violent version of the regal ball and sceptre.

Under the picture are the words "The Pope Knows".

I'm not in the least bit bothered by it.

I can sense the icy wind of change in the air of Lost Hope.

Since the current regime in this miserable little place will not allow me to leave, I can think of only one alternative.

I'm going to have to stage a rebellion.

WEEK 35 DAY 4

I spent yesterday whispering unrest and spreading rumours and I think I successfully planted the seeds of doubt in a few minds.

The difficult thing was choosing the right people to talk to; people I had seen show signs of discontent with the Pope and his overbearing papacy.

Using the backs of anti-Morris posters, I've managed to cobble together some posters of my own.

Simple messages. Basic truths like "The Pope must go" and "Why do what the Pope says?" seem ambiguous enough to spread dissension.

I got talking to an old man with ginger hair. He looked a bit like a geriatric Don Rickles, only with a nervous tic that sent the whole right hand side of his body into spasms. His name was Polo and he claimed he had been in Lost Hope for the last seventy years, and that the Pope had been there long before him.

Clearly this is not true, the Pope I saw couldn't have been much over forty.

I pointed this out to Polo and he started going on about a fountain of youth hidden in the white chamber, a zebra man living in the woods, and the albino water-dragons asleep in the frozen depths of Lake Hell.

To be fair, much of this sounded quite convincing. However, then I made the mistake of asking him how he came by such an unusual name.

He lifted up the ginger hair on the back of his head to show me a fist sized hole where, I suspect, a fair chunk of his brain used to inhabit.

I asked how it had happened and he muttered something about the Pope and a rusty spoon... I didn't press him on the matter.

Polo, the man with the hole in his head.

WEEK 35 DAY 5

My posters already seem to be taking effect.

I've noticed people in conspiratorial huddles all over town. A few have even approached me and told me a few home truths about the Pope.

Apparently he rarely makes public appearances, only sees people one at a time, and does most of his enforcing via a handful of thugs who don't actually live in Lost Hope.

To be honest, not much of this makes much sense to me. Why keep these people here against their will? Why call yourself the "Pope"? Why be sufficiently proud of killing a chipmunk that you would mount its head on the wall?

There is much wrong here.

I marched up to the Pope's front door and hammered on it until my hands hurt (which wasn't very long given the recent abuse they have suffered).

No one answered. Maybe he is out, or maybe he is hiding behind his settee, afraid I will expose him for the fraud he is.

I talked to a number of people after that. People are already coming forward and expressing their desire to leave Lost Hope.

I gave them all some rousing rhetoric and told them to spread the news.

There's a new candidate for the Pope in town - he's good, fair, kind and noble and he's from just west of Market Drayton.

I was talking about me.

WEEK 35 DAY 6

I was caught putting up one of the posters. It was a particularly inflammatory one that suggested the Pope should be lynched, Pope on a rope.

I was taken for another private audience before the Pope. I didn't even have to wait very long this time.

It all went quite well and after the usual death threats and intimidating gestures he offered me a full pardon if I left Lost Hope and went back to Shropshire.

I declined on two counts.

Firstly I feel it is my responsibility to give the people of Lost Hope a chance to taste the sweet free air of the West Midlands before they die.

Secondly, and most importantly, when the Pope suggested I go back home, he used a profanity immediately before the sacred name of my mother county. "..and go back to *&$£ing Shropshire"! he said.

I will not stand for anyone, Pope or no, to show the gleaming fields of Salopia such disrespect.

Now I imagine that the Pope is in fact just another troubled individual in desperate need of a little bit of Shropshire, but this time he had gone too far.

I knew then that this man had to be taught a lesson.

As I was dragged out the front door, a crowd was waiting for me, not an enormous crowd, but big enough to legitimately call a crowd. Not a huddle or a group, not quite a throng but certainly throng-ish, a crowd and they were calling my name.

"morris"

"Morris"

"MORRIS!"

They were calling my name and it wasn't so they could drop me in a lake, or burn me alive. No, it was because they believed in the power of Shropshire, embodied in Mr Morris Telford.

It's time for the reign of Pope Morris.

The men that protected the Pope and did other general thuggish duties took one look at the crowd, got in their four by four and left.

Didn't see them again.

My followers joined me and we went looking for the Pope. It's midnight now and I'm sitting on his throne typing this while the others search for him. Today is the dawn of a new age.

It's time for the reign of Pope Morris.

I'm renaming the town.

It's no longer Lost Hope, it's New Hope. Partly because I have given the people here a reason to hope again, a reason to live again, I've removed the oppressive regime and replaced it with one based on Shropshire values; and partly because it was the name of the first Star Wars film and I think it sounds cool.

WEEK 35 DAY 7

We found the Pope.

He was holed up in a secret room in the left wing. It was a little room with nothing but rolls of toilet paper.

He'd built quite a sturdy little igloo out of them in the middle of the room and was sitting in it quite calmly, humming what was (as far as I could tell) the theme-tune from classic eighties action motorbike TV series Street Hawk.

The people of New Hope wanted to express their frustration at living under his violent rule by beating seventeen shades of suffering out of him, but I managed to stop them.

They did strip him naked and make him dance on broken glass, but this was just preliminary cruelty and after a few hours I got them to listen to me.

I told them that even if they tortured, killed, stuffed and mounted him, it wouldn't undo all the suffering, it would just be causing more suffering.

I don't want to be responsible for that.

My mission is to help people, to expose wrongs, to eat the pie of evil and lies with the knife and fork of goodness and decency... to scrub off the droppings of the bird of injustice from the double-glazing of society... and to get the correct numbers and dialling codes of the Mr Tricksters, Mrs Charlatans and Evildoers Esquires of this world from the great phone directory of perception, give them a call about some home truths and reverse the charges.

I convinced the people to let me have a day alone with him, find out why he set himself up as Pope.

I'm going into a small room with him now.

There's nothing in there either of us can use to hurt each other. It's just me, the ex-Pope tied to a chair, a bottle of water and nothing to do but tell him about Shropshire for the next 24 hours.

I expect he'll tell me everything.

WEEK 36 DAY 1

I just spent twenty-six hours locked in a small room with a mentally unstable pope-fixated megalomaniac.

It was a bit like working weekend overtime in consumables and procurement, (just me and Peter Scholes in a small stationary room for hours and hours), only marginally less stressful.

Peter used to talk about how much he liked trains, train related trivia, train stations, the uniforms people who work on trains wear and the minutiae of train engine configurations.

He had this theory that hidden within the British Rail train timetables were the answers to all the great mysteries of the universe. It was quite blisteringly boring and just got in the way of the important task of counting the paperclips.

So I used the same tactic on the Pope that drove me so mad with Peter Scholes. I talked to him for 25 straight hours about stationary - About paperclips, staples, staplers, catalogues, the subtle differences between different paper qualities, the 1347 varieties of black pen available in the UK, the dichotomy of reusable toner cartridges, the heady complexities of laminate fold over and the bitter beauty to be found in every single box of 125mm bar tags with plastic ends.

The Pope actually broke down after about 19 hours... but I felt I had to finish my point about the European standard paperclip and its superior cousin the British Standard paperclip (and how much the slightest inferiority in the original base mould can change the angle of the upper curve and thus give reduced paper holding ability).

The Pope's real name is Steven Watson. He's a retired civil servant from Devon.

When he finally broke I almost felt sorry for him., After all his posturing and menace, in the end he's really just like anyone else - frightened, alone and in serious need of a dose of Shropshire.

We had a town meeting and it was agreed that with my help, the Pope and twenty of his ex-followers are to come to live in Moreton Say. The rest are staying in New Hope to rebuild their lives, and then, when that doesn't work out, come on to Shropshire later.

WEEK 36 DAY 2

I awoke this morning to a crowd outside my window shouting "Pope Morris".

It was all very nice what with the town women fighting over who would help dress me and make my breakfast, the parade in my honour and the 'pledging of allegiance to Pope Morris and Shropshire ceremony... but I did feel they had taken it all a bit too far when a queue formed to kiss my feet.

Especially with the current state of my blisters.

We set off tomorrow, away from New Hope and on to new, fresh and potentially lethal challenges.

WEEK 36 DAY 3

It's hard going crossing the Alaskan wilderness.

The snowmobiles we found in the Pope's shed are a big help. There's a party atmosphere in the small rag tag fleet following me across the snowscape, the occasional whoop from behind me betrays the barely contained joy that these people feel now they are free... that or their snowmobile went over a rock.

There are some pretty big animals around, bears, wolves and something called the Oor-hupu that apparently looks like a giant grey bear, walks like a man and eats children. So we have taken some of the Pope's firearms with us for protection. Nothing too much, just a few Uzi's, a general electric mini-gun and a bag of grenades.

According to Trent (Our tracker and guide; a six foot three American Indian who had been tied up in the Pope's shed and reminds me of Derek Griffiths in his Playschool heyday), we are two days hard travel from the nearest airport.

It's an old military base and I'm sure it will be full of friendly American servicemen ready to help 22 heavily armed, bearded strangers on snowmobiles.

If I can charter a flight for us from there to Heathrow, it looks like my Mother's funeral might be getting a few extra Alaskan mourners next week.

WEEK 36 DAY 4

Trent tells me that Alaskan people have 357 different words for snow, but not a single one for Bingo.

He also told me that at night the Oor-hupu sing to him in his dreams using quite complex vocal harmonies... and give him recipes for special cakes that, when baked, become sentient and are able to work out the value of Pi to several thousand decimal places.

I jokingly asked him if they gave him a recipe for a special pie that can work out cake to several thousand decimal places, but he didn't respond favourably.

I think when I chose Trent as our guide, I may have made a poor decision based on my own racial stereotyping of the American Indians as expert guides and trackers. Thus forgetting the simple truth that, no matter what race, colour, or religion you belong to, you can still turn out to be a complete nutter.

WEEK 36 DAY 5

Starting to get cold and hungry already. Some of the convoy are complaining about the lack of provisions and questioning my leadership skills.

I pointed out to them in no uncertain terms that I had been on the Leadership Skills workshop with work and was fully qualified to lead groups up to and including 50 people in an office environment.

They didn't seem nearly as impressed as my mother had been when I brought home the certificate. I'd like to see them co-ordinate a team-building exercise with a roomful of bored stationary clerks and come up with the sort of results and enthusiasm I did in the legendary summer of 1993.

Trent suggested eating Steven Watson, but I managed to distract him by showing him how to play solitaire on my palmtop. Apparently Trent had been locked in the Pope's shed for nearly seven years, so it's really no wonder he has a few 'issues'.

The world is full of people with sadness in their lives. Nearly everyone has had, at some point in their time here, something devastating happen to them. However, it's important to maintain perspective.

When my first pet died, I thought my world had shattered. Then I found out that Shropshire wasn't the centre of the civilised world and I had to come to terms with that.

After that my Father came home one day in a dress and announced that he wanted us to call him Aunt Felicity. Then one day at work I accidentally stapled my hand to the desk and on that day I knew the true meaning of pain.

So my point is, I think, that you never know what's around the corner... and what seems like the worst thing ever on Monday may seem relatively trivial next week, after you find out what's going to happen to you on Tuesday afternoon.

I told this to Trent. I told him that even though being locked in a shed for seven years might seem bad now, it will probably seem relatively trivial after he experiences all the other terrible things that life is going to throw at him.

I think I cheered him up.

WEEK 36 DAY 6

It's probably just the exposure to cold and the lack of food, but I could have sworn I heard the lilting melody of a sweet choir coming from the trees last night. It seemed to be saying "…lightly combine the eggs, half a cup of milk and one teaspoon of vanilla. Mix with the dry ingredients and stir well. Add ground cinnamon to taste…"

We should be near the military base now. I'm beginning to doubt it even exists, but we are all committed to believing in Trent now.

I pressed him on the question of exactly where the base was and how he knew about it and he was a little vague. He just said "When the snow eagle dives into the valley of the spirit, the men with fire sticks hide in their tin boxes."

I persisted and after my constant nagging for a couple of hours he added, "Through the ice walls and over the moon's shadow, the wounded wolf always crawls back to the pack." Which again wasn't a great deal of help.

I kept at him. I often find where politeness and courtesy fails, dogged irritation can reap rewards.

After a few hours he ran out of mystic wolf-this and mysterious bear-that and gave in.

"It's seven miles south-south-east," he told me, just before he walked off in a sulk.

WEEK 36 DAY 7

The military base does exist; we can see it now we've passed over a snowy ridge.

I apologised to Trent for doubting him and he clasped me close to his chest, then grabbed my head and pressed his right ear against my left ear. According to his people's traditions this makes us "wax brothers" and we are forever bonded. I like Trent, he reminds me of my Aunt Felicity.

We are approaching the perimeter now. I can see a few soldiers walking their dogs near the large, barbed wire fence, so at least someone is home.

It's been a tough few days but it will all be worth it to see my beloved home once again.

140

If I close my eyes I can see the little round sign at the top of the signpost that says "Moreton Say". Despite the freezing conditions here I can still imagine the warm, silage-tinted Shropshire breeze wafting from the Ostrich farm, past the Moreton Say C of E Controlled Primary School, past Mad George's bungalow, past my Mother hanging out my Star Wars duvet cover to dry on the line and into my hopes and dreams via my figurative nose.

I hope we get a warm welcome from the American military base.

WEEK 37 DAY 1

On reflection, it's been rather an exciting day.

As we sped towards the base, a few of us got a bit over excited at finally finding contact with civilisation, you have to remember that some of these people have been trapped in a pseudo-religious dictatorship for the past few years of their lives and it's the first time they have had contact with the outside world for ages.

This overspill of excitement happened to manifest itself in the waving of arms and whooping.

Those arms were holding guns and when the arms holding the guns waved, the guns tended to wave as well.

The waving of guns was interspersed with the occasional high-spirited gunshot into the air as a sort of polite announcement to the military base that we had arrived.

The arms, waving and occasionally shooting the guns, were attached to burly bearded men on speeding snowmobiles and in retrospect, I can see why an American soldier might jump to the wrong conclusion and perceive us as a potential threat.

There might have been the odd high-spirited grenade too.

So we arrived at the base in a flurry of snow and gunfire, and the American soldiers returned fire, took cover and set their dogs on us.

It was as the dogs were bounding towards us, as their blood red gums and dagger teeth rasping with carefully trained clouds of anger in the Alaskan cold, as the Americans fired random shots at my friends, as the snow sleds turned to a halt and set up a defensive line a bit like the old wagon trains used to in cowboy films, as Trent dove in front of me to cover his wax brother from any harm that I realised my moment had come. This was exactly where and when I was supposed to be.

I might not have had the world changing effect I had intended to have these past 37 weeks, I might not yet be able to address world leaders and give them an interesting half hour presentation with overhead projectors and different lumocolor highlighter pens on how to achieve world peace in three easy steps, I might not have touched everyone yet with the importance of living life the Shropshire way, but right here, right now these people believed in me and I wasn't going to let them down.

I pushed Trent aside and walked across the icy no-mans land between the line of snow sleds and the barbed wire perimeter fence. I held both my hands in the traditional Salopian gesture of peace and goodwill, thumbs extended to the heavens in recognition of the late, great Clive of India's spirit of adventure, index finger and middle finger pointing forward in memory of Thomas Telford's architectural vision and two remaining fingers closed to represent the two values of Shropshire life we hold most dear, honesty and good quality gingerbread.

I do have to admit that to the eye of someone unfamiliar in obscure English hand gestures this might look like I was pretending to wield two imaginary guns.

The important thing is though, that my lone stand, my personal bravery and my complete lack of consideration for my own personal safety sufficiently confused the American military personnel and they stopped shooting.

This gave Trent and the others chance to surrender.

Which is just as well because I was bleeding quite heavily from a bullet that had gone straight through my left shoulder and once I could see that everything was working out just fine I allowed myself to pass out.

I woke up about half an hour ago in a lovely clean white linen bed, with my palmtop in the bag by my side and Trent strapped to a bed just across the room from me. I look forward to asking the doctor when I can charter a flight out of here.

WEEK 37 DAY 2

I'd like to mention how welcoming the American military have been, I'd like to emphasise how much I appreciate the way they have taken us at our word despite our unorthodox arrival and embraced us as world citizens and fellow advocates of the common good.
I'd like to, but I can't, because they've been really quite unpleasant.

Not only do they refuse to arrange my safe passage back to Shropshire, but also they have told me all sorts of things about my friends. Some of which I suspect may be fabricated.

Trent is strapped down on some sort of sack truck in a manner not unlike that of Anthony Hopkins in those sheep films and is being shipped to Nestle headquarters where he is wanted regarding a multi million pound cake recipe fraud case.

Lost Hope was not Steven Watson's first attempt at megalomania; he is wanted for an incident in 1989 when he convinced an entire town in Virginia that he was the reincarnation of Caesar Augustus. He ruled them for three years, was going to lead the world into a new age of prosperity and fun with the people of Lynchburg as world leaders, but after they built a coliseum, an eighty foot high statue of him wearing a toga and renamed the town "Watsonville", he left with all their life savings. I guess he must have used the funds to set up Lost Hope. The funny thing is, the people of Watsonville still believe in him, they have annual chariot races, call all their firstborn sons Steven (and the girls Stephanie) and line the streets every Thursday awaiting his triumphant return. "Watson Thursday" they call it, which oddly enough is exactly what my Mother used to ask when I was flicking through the Radio Times on a Wednesday evening. The FBI, CIA, NSA and probably lots of other people in suits with concealed weapons have been looking for him for years.

Another of our number, a quiet but disturbingly twitchy individual called Bacon who looks like he's constantly getting electric shocks, is apparently an eighty seven year old Soviet scientist. They say he holds the key to an ecologically friendly renewable energy source that would make petrol, diesel and oil obsolete and so several major car-manufacturing companies have a price on his head.

Worst of all, they checked me against their files and say I am wanted in several countries for crimes against society, incitement to riot, false advertising, monk confusing and littering. All nonsense of course.

WEEK 37 DAY 3

The Americans injected me with some sort of truth serum this morning, which actually had no effect whatsoever on me, as I always endeavour to be truthful. They asked me what I was doing here and I told them, in no uncertain terms, and at great length all about my life quest, Shropshire, bingo and Countdown.

They left to check bbc.co.uk and see if it was all true.

I hope they read the archive, some of it's quite good.

WEEK 37 DAY 4

Not much to report today.

Just lots of questions from the military. They tied me down for a bit, threatened me with humiliation, electrocution and something else I can't mention as my Aunt Felicity might read this. A man in a black suit and dark sunglasses kept taking pictures of it all with a small digital camera.

Interestingly, they attached electrodes to Trent and tried to use shock treatment but it didn't work, no current seemed to pass through him. Trent attributes this to his diet consisting mainly of cakes, not known for their conductive properties.

WEEK 37 DAY 5

The sky outside is taunting me, I can see clouds freewheel past, I imagine them continuing on to Mother Shropshire and wafting gently over the children playing on the Wrekin.

Will I never get home to Moreton Say?

The vicar will be terribly disappointed if I miss my own Mother's funeral.

I remember once when I was a young boy, the local prophet, Bruce Foresight, grabbed me by the shoulders, looked me in the eyes and cheerily said, "You'll die in a cold place without your Mother". I wonder if this is what he meant?

To be fair, Bruce also told me once, "Mark my words, one day you'll be King of Spain and have a thousand wives." and on another occasion, "Before the moon is full again, the streets of Telford will run red with the blood of the badger men." So I never gave his portents much heed.

WEEK 37 DAY 6

We staged a beautifully crafted escape today.

Imagine the blockbuster film Con Air, although with less gratuitous violence, more convincing dialogue and the Nicholas Cage character played by a Countdown fan with a Shropshire accent.

Trent staged a seizure. He has an uncanny ability to foam at the mouth like a rabid dog, he says all he has to do is imagine eating an underdone Victoria Sponge made with poor quality ingredients and it sends him into a frenzy. So we called the guards, who unstrapped Trent while the rest of us nipped out the door. Then a couple of us nipped back in, there were some thumping sounds and Trent came with us too. It was all very violent and not at all the way I would have liked to do it, but they left us no choice.

Then, as luck and foolish secret military base design would have it, there was an aircraft hanger full of exciting looking planes just next door to the infirmary, we picked one with silver wings and flew straight through the hanger doors, then we all got out and picked another plane because we had just broken the first one driving it through some metal doors.

And then we simply flew off to freedom, soaring into the sky like a greased Frisbee.

WEEK 37 DAY 7

Conditions on the plane are quite good. We found a Jacuzzi in one of the upper levels, there's tuxedo's for everyone and enough champagne to intoxify the whole of Shropshire.

Fortunately, one of our number, a wiry Texan called Phil Newman, who has some sort of skin condition that makes him look like an inside out Clare Raynor, is an excellent pilot and is heading, as best he can, towards Shropshire. Although his navigating skills seem to consist of looking out the window a lot and asking people where the sun is.

The plane has all sorts of gadgetry on board and is conveniently invisible to radar, very handy for crossing international airspace.

Trent found a flight manual in the cockpit, apparently the plane is called "air force one" which struck me as a very pedestrian name so we re-christened her "Morris One" and aimed for Shropshire.

I'm going home.

WEEK 38 DAY 1

Phil, our self-appointed pilot and navigator, appears to have gone to the school of aviation as Icarus.

He's under the impression that all the dials and switches and little flashing lights that litter the cockpit are for novice pilots, and that all he needs is a compass and a general idea of windspeed.

I'm a great believer in letting people fulfill their potential, but even in my most optimistic moments, I'd be hard pressed to entrust my life to someone who thinks they can successfully gauge the windspeed of 50 tons of high-tech high-speed winged metal with pinpoint accuracy just by licking their finger and popping it outside for a bit.

This cavalier attitude makes me uneasy, but there's no escape from the frivolity. The men have found some video games in one of the rooms and are playing Space Harrier with the volume turned up far too loud, which to be quite honest is jangling my nerves a bit.

This isn't helped by Phil doing barrel rolls every time someone gets a high score.

I'm going for a lie down.

WEEK 38 DAY 2

Phil made an announcement just now on the tannoy. He asked us to look out the window "to see the shores of the Thames".

I had to go up to the cockpit personally to tell him that while the UK sports some lovely beaches, some of which are almost completely free of radiation and sewage, none of these lovely beaches are quite that big, or have camels on them, or indeed, pyramids. After half an hour of arguing, Phil conceded that we probably were over Egypt after all and stopped looking for Big Ben casting it's shadow over the Nile.

It was while we were arguing that Phil knocked a button on a hitherto untouched control panel and a screen lit up with all sorts of satellite navigation, GPS and hologramatic navigational sensors. It was very impressive and looks to all intents and purposes like an expensive special effect. I clicked a few icons, entered the postcode for my house in Moreton Say and clicked the "auto-navigation" button. The plane banked sharply to the right and steadied, a little message lit up in reassuring green that said "Course Locked".

Phil wasn't very happy, but I managed to distract him by telling him that we'd found a sea-lion in one of the Jacuzzis. By the time he realised it was just Trent having a bubble bath I'd locked him in.

WEEK 38 DAY 3

We hit some turbulance in the night, I think a bit of the plane dropped off, I hope it wasn't anything important. Like a wing.

Phil got loose again and tried to take control of the plane. One of the Alaskans, a tall man called Obican Rumus with long silver-white hair and a painted nails, thought it was a good idea to keep Phil from the controls, so he locked the door to the cockpit and threw the key down the toilet. Unfortunately no-one was in the cockpit at the time.

After three hours of trying to fish the key out with some string and a magnet, I gave up. Although I did manage to retrieve a gold tooth, a pair of cufflinks that were inscribed "The Gipper", a tiny, beautifully detailed, diecast toy soldier and a coin marked "One American Dollar" dated 2023. The coin had the image of George W. Bush on it, but he looked much older, had an eyepatch and what looked like a mobile phone but may have been a cybernetic ear.

So the plane is on autopilot and we have no way of getting into the cockpit. I'm just hoping that among the satellite navigation, GPS and hologramatic navigational sensors, there's also something that automatically lands the plane.

WEEK 38 DAY 4

Things are actually getting quite bad now. Steven Watson bailed out a few minutes ago, he wailed something about "sensing Devon" and make a break for it. He grabbed a parachute and was out the escape hatch before we could stop him. Trent tried to follow him but five of us managed to hold him down while the hatch was secured. I have to admire Trent for trying to leap out of a speeding plane wearing only a bathrobe and fluffy yellow slippers, he must really hate the ex-Pope.

Despite everything Steven Watson did, I hope he's OK and lands on something relatively soft.

I must admit, just before he jumped out of the plane, I did sense a nearby evil, a terrible chill of foreboding, like the Shrewsbury marathon running over my grave, so maybe we really are over Devon. The one and only good thing about Devon is, it's relatively near Shropshire, so I actually hope Steven was right, it means I'm nearly home.

The plane is juddering and some of the men are talking about jumping out. I counted the parachutes and we are one short. I haven't said anything to the men, it's my fault they are here, I'll go last.

WEEK 38 DAY 5

Morris One seems to be circling, and it has been for most of the night. The floor is constantly tilted at about 30 degrees, which makes drinking from a glass surprisingly difficult.

I've wedged myself between the back of a seat and some sort of storage locker while I type this, a few of the men are trying to break into the cockpit. One of the Alaskans jumped out a few minutes ago, I hope he remembered his parachute.

If this is the last time I send an entry in from my palmtop, then goodbye and remember – I did it all for Shropshire…..

WEEK 38 DAY 6

…

WEEK 38 DAY 7

…

WEEK 39 DAY 1

I think I'm dead.

I awoke a few minutes ago, I'm dressed in a pair of familiar, faded Dangermouse pyjamas, and I'm lying in what looks very much like my old bed, with my old Star Wars duvet and my collection of Bingo Markers stacked, labelled and hermetically sealed in their special containers just under the photo of Carol Voderman.

Mother came in just now with a tray. Scrambled egg on toast, a cup of sweet tea and a little gingerbread man with a smiling face.

Just the way I like it.

All as it should be.

Except last time I checked, I was in a inside a stolen plane, plummeting towards certain death, my mother was dead and I'm sure I threw away my Dangermouse pyjamas sometime during the mid nineties.

I'm both confused and hungry. I'm going to eat something.

I have eaten my scrambled egg, toast and gingerbread.

I have drunk my tea.

It was very nice, although the crusts had been cut from my toast. I always used to eat my toast sans crust, but I tried asking for the waitress to cut the crusts from my toast once in a roadside diner in Birmingham, America, early on in my travels. She looked at me as if she had just popped a Werther's original in her mouth and forgotten to take the wrapper off, and suggested cutting off something else entirely. So over the past few months of hard travelling I have grown accustomed to taking my toast straight, and coping with whatever crusts life threw at me, both figurative and literal.

Mother always used to cut the crusts from my toast though, and it's this attention to the little details, like the crusts, like the stain on my duvet just over Han Solo's blaster, like the crack in the bedroom window where the badger dropped from the sky, like the loose floorboard under which I keep the bingo marker reputedly used by Sir Thomas Telford himself in the Bingo marathon of 1893 that concern me. If this was, as I first thought, some sort of elaborate copy of my bedroom created by the Americans or the military or Country Life, then I would notice subtle things wrong with it, but it's absolutely perfect in every tiny detail.

Except my Mother is here, and my pyjamas are here, and that's impossible.

So I must be dead, and heaven looks exactly like Shropshire, which really just confirms what I've been saying all along.

WEEK 39 DAY 2

I'm not dead.

It turns out there is a more rational explanation.

The plane did crash, but we had two important factors in our favour. It had run out of fuel, so we didn't explode, and we crashed into the swamp that extends from my old back garden to the edge of the Bletchley Road, which lessened the impact of the impact. To illustrate, try dropping a marble into some thick soup, or a trifle, or some mushy peas, or a tub of hair gel, or now I come to think of it, try dropping a marble into some swamp. Then try dropping the same marble onto a concrete floor. You'll see how important the swamp factor was in our landing.

From my bedroom window I can see the last of Morris One's fuselage slowly sinking into the marshy ground just behind the greenhouse, like Artax in the Neverending Story, conveniently and completely destroying any evidence that I borrowed a luxury jet. Yet again, Shropshire provides.

My Mother is alive. It turns out she faked her own death so I would come home. Which, when you think about it, is perfectly rational behaviour for a loving Mother who misses her little poppet.

And I did throw away my Dangermouse pyjamas in 1996, but Mother retrieved them from the bin bag.

WEEK 39 DAY 3

At first I was angry that my Mother had faked her death. Angry that she had lied to me, angry that she had concocted an elaborate story that made me blame myself for her death, angry that she didn't let me do my own thing.

Then she told me she had recorded every single episode of Countdown I'd missed while I was away and to be honest, with the thought of all those unwatched hours of conundrums awaiting me, it was hard to stay angry.

Even using long play, she used sixteen E180 VHS tapes.

WEEK 39 DAY 4

Jim Hawkins of BBC Shropshire interviewed me today, my words will be going out on the airwaves to the good people of Shropshire, and I expect a significant media frenzy following the broadcast.

I may have rambled a bit on the radio show, I remember pointing out that even the gravel in Moreton Say seems that bit more special then the gravel anywhere else. It was just the excitement of media attention, the professional studio, the complimentary cup of percolated coffee and the little visitors badge that said "Morris Telford – BBC". I could feel the buzz of excitement in the radio studios as I arrived, the receptionist greeted me with just the slightest hint of what can only be described as reverential awe.

I've arrived on the local Radio scene and the world is once again my oyster.

From now on I'm Mr Action, Mr Go-Getting-Day-Seizing-Super-Achiever, Mr Man of the Hour.

Morris Telford – Media Dynamo.

WEEK 39 DAY 5

Spent the day watching Countdown.

20 episodes back to back, one after the other, a non-stop Countdownathon. It was one of the happiest days of my life.

It's funny, when you watch Countdown in bulk like that, you can tell which episodes are filmed in groups. For a few episodes Carol's hair will look one way, then it will change for the next few and so on, it was quite fascinating. I wrote a brief Email to Channel 4 suggesting they re-run old episodes of Countdown back to back all day every Wednesday, I'm sure it would boost the ratings.

During the salad years, when I was saving up, preparing for my Salopian Odyssey, I fashioned a rudimentary life size replica of the Countdown studio out of farmyard machinery and scarecrows. The big clock was made from the flywheel of a combine harvester, the desks were bales of hay, the scoreboard I borrowed from a local cricket club and I spent ages altering some scarecrows to look like Carol Vorderman, Richard Whiteley and Richard Stilgoe. Well, I spent ages altering some scarecrows to look like Carol Vorderman and Richard Whiteley.

WEEK 39 DAY 6

After spending all yesterday watching Countdown, I dreamed about Countdown, I dreamed of a world where every corner was dictionary corner, every woman looked like Carol and on the hour, every hour the church clock rang out the countdown theme tune – "Da-da da-da diddly-dum…. Doooo!".

It was beautiful.

Watched more Countdown today too.

To be fair though, I had to watch Countdown, I can't go out. As an expression of her love for me, my Mother has hidden my passport and locked me in my bedroom. She isn't very keen on me setting off again to change the world. When I say she isn't very keen, if I start to talk about travelling again she puts her hands over her ears and starts screeching "Mother can't hear you" in a sing-song harpy lilt that makes my teeth itch.

Talking of teeth, Aunt Felicity just got back from the dentists. Aunt Felicity suffers with 'dry sockets', which is only slightly more unpleasant than it sounds. I'm not sure if they actually re-moisten the sockets at the dentists or just fill them in, but I do know that it affects everything that Aunt Felicity says for the week or two after the dentist appointment.

WEEK 39 DAY 7

Trent, Obican and the remaining Alaskans came round again this morning and interrupted Countdown.

Aunt Felicity answered the door, when they asked if I was in I could hear through the gap under my bedroom door that she was trying to say "Yes, come in, he's in his room", but it came out as a sort of strangled, retarded sound and they left presuming it was some local dialect they were unfamiliar with.

I'm sure they'll be fine anyway, I've bought them a barn and they are equipping it with items salvaged from Morris One. They will soon have one of the few barn conversions in the area to boast a Jacuzzi, a home cinema, an inflatable staircase, an open fireplace built from a converted jet engine and enough complimentary peanuts to last nine lifetimes.

I'm going to break out tomorrow, but while I'm here I may as well watch the rest of the Countdown tapes.

Da-da da-da diddly-dum Doooo.

WEEK 40 DAY 1

First thing this morning, I tied together some old shirts, let them down from my bedroom window and shimmied down them like a polyester Rapunzel. The first licks of the suns rays were tentatively caressing the silage tower, the birds were welcoming the new dawn with open wings and Aunt Felicity could be heard from the front bedroom rasping and snoring through dry sockets.

I'm sitting on the bus now, on my way to Market Drayton, the Mecca of gingerbread and Muller dairy deserts. It's seems like a lifetime ago that I last walked down Queen Street and marvelled at the diversity of folk that reside here.

I'm really looking forward to it.

The bus just passed the Muller yoghurts factory. Ludwig Muller started out in Bavaria in the late 19th century, and although it took the company over a century of scouring every corner of the earth for the perfect dairy dessert making location, they finally settled on Market Drayton. They could have gone anywhere in the world, and there are certainly cheaper places to make yoghurt, but no, they chose Market Drayton.

Why? Because the Mullers were called here by forces they could not control. Forget Wall Street, cast aside thoughts of International Stock Exchanges, and don't bother with silly old Silicon Valley. Market Drayton is the very epicentre of commercial and manufacturing success. For thousands of years people have congregated in this, the ultimate Market Town to make, buy and sell the most marvellous of arcane and wonderful products, from ages ago when men exchanged the secrets of the wheel and fire here, to the industrial revolution when Market Drayton saw the first steam powered bicycles, to the present day when master craftsmen like Rupert Usermanual and Martha Etigran sell their unique creations in the local market.

No wonder they decided to make Yogz and Muller Rice here too.

I'll be there soon in the thick of it all, with a spring in my step, £32.46 to spend and 8 shopping hours until teatime.

WEEK 40 DAY 2

It's the most commonplace things about Shropshire that I think I've missed the most. The landscape, the air, the people and, of course, the bakeries.

I've travelled all around the world, tasted delicacies from exotic kitchens, seen unimaginable vistas, befriended all manner of folk, danced with seventeen shades of death, and remained relatively unmoved.

Yesterday I went to Market Drayton and ate some freshly baked gingerbread that had been amusingly crafted into the shape of a footballer. It moved me to tears.

Not only did the gingerbread crumble with the delicate softness unrivalled even by the silken thigh of Andrex, the goddess of softness, but it skipped that fine line between sweetness and spice that only a tenth dan gingerbread baker, benefiting from over 200 years of gingerbread baking lore could achieve.

I fell to my knees in the middle of the street and shouted my thanks to the late, great Roland Lateward, grandfather of gingerbread making, entrepreneur and regional winner of the 1789 "amusing cake" Olympics.

You might think to yourself that I was over-reacting to what was, after all, just some flour, sugar, shortening, cinnamon, ground ginger, baking powder, salt, baking soda, vanilla extract and eggs. If you could have been there, if you could have tasted what I tasted, you'd have been there next to me, on your knees, stopping traffic, shouting till your lungs ached "Thankyou, Roland Lateward, Thankyou."

As I explained to the police later on, and again to Mother as she came to get me, with gingerbread of that quality, no reaction could ever be categorised as an overreaction.

I spent today watching the last of my Countdown backlog, and while I was obviously misty eyed as the final credits rolled on the last tape, it also gave me a sense of release and freedom, as there's nothing else really urgent keeping me here. The world needs me. If I close my eyes I can imagine the chatter of thousands of desperate souls wishing aloud that a man would walk into their lives and show them exactly where the juicy peach of happiness really is.

I am that man and Shropshire is that juicy peach.

WEEK 40 DAY 3

Mother is still refusing to tell me where my passport is.

I know she means well but as I've explained to her, the world needs me. She might need me to protect the house from burglars, terrorists and Devon folk, to cut the grass, clean the gutters and unscrew jar lids, but the world needs me to bring it enlightenment, show it the error of it's ways and point it in the direction of Shropshire.

Still, even if I can't go abroad, there are still plenty of places that need to know about Shropshire. When you think about it, there must be people in other parts of Great Britain that see Shropshire on the television all the time but never think to come here. Why is that? Why if you were sat at home in one of the lesser counties and saw the solid majesty of the Wrekin or the coming together of the many creative strands that is the Ludlow festival or the sheer, unadulterated marvellousness of Ironbridge, would you not immediately run from your house and head for Shropshire to start a new life amongst these marvels?

Why? I just don't understand. I have come across a few in my travels that, like a man in the desert dying of thirst refusing a nice cold glass of iced water, have spurned my message, ignored my important information about Shropshire being the best place ever and gone on living their blinkered little lives.

Maybe I need to be more direct.

WEEK 40 DAY 4

I tried one last time to get Mother to give me my passport. I convinced Trent to dress up as a policeman and demand that my Mother provide some identification for me.

To be fair to Trent, he really got into character, and made good use of the traditional "evening all" greeting accompanied by the bobbing of knees and nodding of head. Unfortunately Mother knows that we don't have any local bobby's that are six foot three American Indians who look a bit like Derek Griffiths in his Playschool heyday.

She sent him packing; literally, she made him some sandwiches, a slice of cake and a flask of tea for the journey back to his barn, which was particularly thoughtful of her since it's only ten minutes walk down the road.

WEEK 40 DAY 5

Toby came round to see me today, he tells me that Sophia is expecting their child very shortly, she would have come too but she didn't.

I can see that Toby looks up to me as the man that turned his life around. My gut reaction was to emphasise that all the changes he has made in his life have been thanks to his own determination, resolve and application, but he won me round and I found myself agreeing with him that yes, I was solely responsible for his good fortune lately. He's got a good job, a good home, a beautiful partner, a baby on the way, and he lives in Moreton Say. What more could anyone want? He is very lucky he met me, but then I'm very lucky I met him, he was my first real success and I feel quite paternal towards him, he's like the son I never had with the girlfriend I never had.

Toby tried to offer me all sorts of stuff to show his appreciation. He offered me money, he offered me a car, he offered to set me up with a friend of Sophia's, he even offered to name his firstborn child after me, but I refused. I don't need more money, I can't drive, I'm not interested in Sophia's friends and although Morris is a bold and noble name that any child would be glad to carry, I declined that offer too since Toby's surname is Minor and Sophia's surname is Dancer.

One thing Toby did say in passing was that Mr Magson is on holiday again, somewhere in the sub-continent, and he has a casual vacancy for a stationary clerk. I offered my temporary services and so I start tomorrow.

WEEK 40 DAY 6

I'm back among the safe, familiar and magical world of office consumables. I'm sitting now at a little desk surrounded by a rising forest of unopened stationary orders and I couldn't be happier.

It's only a temporary position, I'm just here to help Toby out and get a taste of my former life, I just wanted to briefly drink once more from the crystal waters of the office stationary lake, to see the lady of the lake hold up a heavy duty Excalibur paperclip for me, so I could once again take my rightful place on the throne of A4 laser copier paper as prince of paperclips, king of consumables.

There is actually quite a large backlog of work here, since Toby got promoted, a string of unsuitable individuals ill-equipped for the heady, high-level responsibilities of my old job, have tried and failed to keep up with the cut and thrust of juggling the many facets of maintaining an organised stationary and consumables section.

 I feel it may take more than a week to get things in shape here and working as well as it was when I left, but I've already filled a whiteboard with spider charts, gant charts and cross-referenced progression plans.

WEEK 40 DAY 7

I got sacked.

It wasn't entirely my fault, although I will admit that some of my proposed changes to the stationary budget were quite radical.

I've become accustomed to thinking on a grander scale since my travels abroad, and it seemed like a good idea at the time to think ahead and order cutting edge technology and to order in bulk. Apparently by the time the finance section noticed my order forms and started cancelling them, I'd already spent the next five years worth of stationary budget, all the company profits for the next two years and the best part of the kitty for the staff Christmas do. On the bright side though, they won't be running out of paperclips until sometime in the 30th century.

I also stayed late last night, very late, and reorganised all seventeen of the offices so that in each room, each desk forms part of a larger circle of desks facing inwards like an office based Knights of the Round Table. This way there will be no more staff facing walls, no more managers sitting isolated away from their staff, and no more arguments over who gets the window seat. Now no one gets the window seat.

I did have to remove a few desks to achieve the circular seating structure, but I think anyone who worked in my new environment would agree it is much preferable to the previous accommodation arrangements.

Toby's boss didn't agree, he sacked me, and worse still, he suspended Toby for employing me. Apparently the company had me on their books as a marked man, never to be employed again, but Toby put my name down as Maurice Letford so the computer didn't pick up on the name.

I feel quite bad about that. I'm sure they will see the funny side in a few days and reinstate him. Walking home with Toby, with the birds playfully darting around overhead, the grass dancing in the summer breeze, the distant contented moos of the Muller cows, the Shropshire sun shining softly on the silage shafts it was quite hard to be depressed about it all, although Toby was having a good try at it.

I'm going to help Toby break the news to Sophia and perhaps explain to her about all my stationary innovations and the lack of management forward thinking.

Now I've never actually met Sophia in person before and I was a little trepidacious at the prospect of seeing her perfect Felicity Kendal nose balanced under those dark blue eyes, but when she opened the door I was shocked. Not in a bad way, just shocked at how large she was, and how she was still utterly beautiful.

I wanted to tell her she was a vision of fruitful womanhood, an earth mother, a splendid consummation of hormones and oestrogen wrapped up in a bountiful baby factory. I wanted to tell Sophia that she was ripe and marvellous.

Before I got chance to tell her any of this, she pushed me firmly but gently aside and asked Toby to get the car.

She was, it turns out, in labour.

It's all very exciting, I'm in the car with them both now and we are nearly at Whitchurch Hospital, I insisted that I come and help, bringing a new life into the world can't be easy and I'm sure I'll be able to offer some advice and guidance at this crucial time.

WEEK 41 DAY 1

I'm waiting in the waiting room at Whitchurch Hospital.

It's very nice, clean, white with tasteful art prints dotted around, a fish tank and three year's worth of OK! and Hello! Magazines. There's also that unmistakable aura of death and hopelessness that I have come to associate with Devon, and yet here I am, still in Shropshire. It doesn't seem right.

Sophia is still in labour. I offered a number of times to assist with the delivery, I was ready to encourage her when to, and when not to push, and I'd prepared a calming little poem about epidurals to recite. Then Sophia grabbed my arm with the sort of grip you can only refuse with the aid of a crowbar and a blowtorch and explained to me all about privacy, families and restraining orders.

I decided they would be better off without me and left them alone.

There's a little TV in the corner of the waiting room, it's been showing the Olympics now for what seems like several days, but can't infact be much more than 3 or 4 hours. There's a lot of nonsense about Athens being the "birthplace of the Olympics" As every well-informed Salopian knows, the Olympics originated in Much Wenlock, when William Penny Brookes had a dream about people of all nationalities competing athletically against each other for gingerbread medallions. Baron Pierre de Coubertain came round for tea and cake at Bill's house one day, pinched his idea, swapped the gingerbread for Bronze, Silver and Gold, moved it from Much Wenlock playing fields to Athens and the rest is history.

It's the same old story, all good things come from Shropshire, but people don't want to believe that a little English county could be responsible for so much, they'd rather believe the forked tongue of the media serpent.

They'd rather believe that Alexander Fleming discovered Penicillin in 1928, when actually George Rumsfold, an unemployed baker from Wellington first discovered it in 1925 while trying out new gingerbread preserving methods. They'd rather think that Samuel Colt invented the revolver in 1846, getting his idea while watching the wheel of a sailing ship, when infact as early as 1820 they were using six shooters in Ludlow to keep marauders from Devon away from the livestock. Samuel Colt visited Ludlow as a teenager on a camping holiday with his parents and bought a model of a revolver from a gift shop next to Ludlow castle, took it to America and put his name to it.

I've met people that still genuinely imagine that Neil Armstrong was the first man on the moon in 1969, when everyone in Moreton Say knows it was really Reginald "Lone" Granger that first set foot there at 10:30am on the 15th of June 1973. Neil's whole "one small step" fiasco was filmed in a disused Laundromat in Washington DC. If you look carefully at some of the footage you can see a tumble dryer poking out from behind a moon rock.

People will believe anything if it's told to them often enough, sometimes I wonder what the world would do without me to smash open the padlock of falsehood that chains shut the rusty gates of propaganda, so they can once again frolic in the garden of hidden truth.

The nurse just came through. Sophie has had the baby.

WEEK 41 DAY 2

Inside the maternity ward, they have cheered up the place with stencils of Disney characters, children's television programmes and a whole wall with nothing but little pictures of people sewing, spinning wheels, thread, and sewing machines. I asked about the mural and one of the nurses explained it was all a mix up with a local artist, they had asked for a wall mural with a "Fimbles" theme. I'm sitting in front of a lovely mural of a giant six fingered hand with an eye in the palm and a different coloured thimble on each finger as I type this on my trusty palmtop and reflect on the serious nature of life, death and birth.

Outside the rain is raining, as it often does. It's early in the morning and I have just had the most tremendous experience of my entire life. I'm aware that I keep saying that, that each time I experience something wonderful it pips the last "most tremendous" moment and becomes the all-new most tremendous moment. Well, it does, and it has and it is.

I just met a brand new Salopian.

Toby and Sophia's new little girl, she looks just like a very, very, very young felicity Kendal.

After Sophia, Toby, the midwife, the other midwife, a couple of nurses, a doctor and a cleaner, I was the ninth person that the little girl saw. She looked like a freshly baked little person, soft and warm from the womb.

I felt very protective of her and very emotional, since Toby would never have met Sophia if it hadn't been for me, this little girl is the nearest I've ever come to a child of my own and if it wasn't for my responsibilities enlightening the rest of humanity, I'd stick around and buy her a pony and a Fisher Price bingo set.

The more I looked down at the innocent, inquisitive, slightly puffy, tiny new eyes, the more I was sure that I need to set off again, so that every baby gets the same chance that lucky little lady has, the chance to taste the sweet air of Shropshire. She gets it by accident of birth, but right now there are children being born in far off countries, there are even poor little souls being born in Devon, that need me out there, letting people know about Shropshire, the Shropshire way of life, and the betterment that awaits them over the rainbow in Moreton Say.

WEEK 41 DAY 3

Sophia comes home later today, so Toby and I are getting the house ready for her homecoming. I suggested a live brass band, a bouncy castle, fireworks and a small but tasteful parade of local people, maybe one or two floats to celebrate Sophia coming back with the baby.

Toby prefers a lower key approach so we have opted for a bunch of flowers, a card and a bit of a tidy up instead. Toby keeps explaining to me how important it is for Sophia to get plenty of rest and how she needs to be left alone for a while, so I've made sure no-one can come and disturb her by setting up my camp bed near the door.

I've already had to explain to Trent, my Mother, Aunt Felicity and a man selling dusters that Sophia will be home soon and needs some space with just her, the baby and Toby.

Some people can be so inconsiderate.

WEEK 41 DAY 4

Sophia came home yesterday evening and got quite emotional when she saw Toby. Then she got even more emotional when she saw me.

I always imagined that when I first met Sophia it would be more magical, much calmer than it's turned out.

I had a phone call from Meat in Australia. Meat has regained his grasp of the English language and is now doing a surprisingly successful job running Morris Telford's Clip, Paper and Staplers in Perth, Australia. He was ringing to tell me that the company is doing incredibly well, they went multi-national last month and still send out a map showing where Moreton Say is with every order.

Sometimes I feel like some modern day King Midas, everything I touch turns to gold. Like a transcendental version of Percy Thrower, everything I'm involved in blossoms and sprouts and grows into something wonderful. As Bruce Foresight said to me this morning, my hands are fertile, my breath is life, my smile a toothy arc of brilliance spreading good cheer and happiness, and wherever my feet take me, there people will rejoice and sing.

I like Bruce.

The great thing is, Meat tells me that Morris Telford's Clip, Paper and Staplers has been buying up smaller companies as they expand their business, and it turns out that my old company, the one that sacked me and Toby last week, is actually owned by MTCP&S. So effectively, I sacked myself last week without knowing it.

As chairman, I've Emailed a minute to Meat outlining a few necessary changes to operations at our Shropshire branch. I've given Toby his job back, with a raise and a promotion, he does have a family to support after all, and I have given out a hefty cash bonus to Theresa who used to buy me Jammie Dodgers.

I've also relocated Mr Magson so he gets to do my old job ordering the paperclips, that'll be a nice surprise for him when he gets back from the sub-continent.

I asked Mother if she was prepared to give me my passport now.

She said no.

WEEK 41 DAY 5

Inspired by Toby cleaning up for Sophia, I had a bit of a tidy up at home, and went straight to the place where my Mother had hidden my passport. It was down the back of the settee, which is, of course, the first place you should always look when you lose something, but often the last place you actually do. I also found a pair of slightly worn, latex pointed ears, a copy of "The Catcher In The Rye", a receipt from the chemists dated 1997 showing that Mother had bought some soap and some growth hormones, the remote control for a Betamax video recorder, a local newspaper clipping with the headline "Shropshire man first on Moon!" and some paperclips. I pocketed the paperclips, you never know when you might need them.

Nothing else is stopping me from setting off again to change the world, so I packed my things, and went to say my goodbyes.

Trent and the other Alaskans weren't at their barn; a note said they've gone to a car boot in Telford to see if they could sell some American military secrets.

Aunt Felicity is at the dentists having her sockets moistened.

Mother went out this morning to see a local sculptor/builder about getting a statue of me commissioned, she isn't back yet. His name is Kenn and he specialises in cement life-size images, apparently he did a very good Henry Walford Davies for the Church Fete last year. She may not want me to go, but I like to think that she must be proud of what I've achieved if she's getting a statue done in my honour.

So there's no-one to give me a send off, no ticker tape parade of adulation, no cheering crowd chanting my name, no placards or banners or specially printed "Good Luck Morris" T-shirts, not even a couple of tearful local beauties clinging to my legs.

It's probably for the best this way, if I slip out quietly without any upset.

The light is on at Toby's next door; I'm going to see if he's in.

WEEK 41 DAY 6

Toby wasn't in last night, he has taken his new little girl for a ride in the car while Sophia, exhausted, got some much needed rest. So it was unfortunate that I chose this particular moment to ring the doorbell.

It's funny, but as she opened the door to me, I realised that it was the first time I'd ever been alone with Sophia. Even though she answered the door tired and irritable, having just fallen asleep for the first time in 50 hours, I couldn't help but smile when I saw it was she.

I didn't have to say anything, it was just nice to see her again, see she was all right before I left, so I just mumbled an apology and told her to let Toby know I had to go liberate some more people from the shackles of ignorance.

To her credit, she was really nice to me. She didn't bring up the fact I'd disturbed her rest, or mention my over enthusiastic offers of help during her recent childbirth, or that I'd just got Toby sacked from her job. She just thanked me for all I'd done and she smiled and she kissed me on my left cheek just on the cheekbone, just under my eye.

I want to say it was like a butterfly, newly emerged from it's chrysalis had chosen my cheek as the first thing it's delicate perfect legs ever landed on, or that it was like brushing against a goddess in a crowded room and feeling for that brief moment of contact what it must be like to be perfect. I want to say that but to be honest it was just a kiss, just her lips on my cheek, just exactly precisely the sort of goodbye I'd wanted.

It occurred to me I should have told Sophia about Toby getting his job back, but I'd rather she thought Toby did it off his own back anyway. He's her partner; her baby's father and I want them so much to be happy together.

I bumped into Toby just now, this morning, as I waited for the bus, he wound the window down and we talked. He let me look in at the baby in her car seat. I told him how I'd bumped into Sophia and how, although we had kissed it was purely platonic and he had nothing to worry about. He laughed and told me they'd named the little girl; they've called her Felicity, after my Father.

WEEK 41 DAY 7

It's excrementally late.

I've spent the day in Market Drayton making travel arrangements.

Now I'm sitting at the coach station, waiting to once more travel south down the A41 to unknown climates, trying to avoid eye contact with the skinhead sitting opposite me. There's something inherently intimidating about a skinhead, stripped to the waist, face painted like a Union Jack, with a Swastika tattooed on their stomach, but I know I shouldn't judge by appearances, I might even like her if I got to know her.

It's exactly the sort of challenge I regularly face in my daily struggle to bring the new dawn of the age of Shropshire to a world darkened by petty rivalries and selfish misunderstanding.

Should I cast aside my preconceptions and embrace humanity one by one, thinking the best of everyone until they prove otherwise, or should I take the discretionary route and choose my battles carefully? Should I hide in the rock face until the birds of possible violence swoop by me or should I wave my arms and shout loudly for the first passing stranger in the hope they will be quite nice? Should I be a wallflower in the dance of life for the tunes of circumstance I am unfamiliar with, or should I grab a random partner and dance the dance of the determined traveller until I drop?

On this occasion I'm going to securely hide my palmtop, pretend to be asleep and hope the skinhead isn't getting on the same coach as me.

Follow **Morris Telford's** continuing **Salopian Odyssey** on the

B B C **Shropshire Website**

Acknowledgements-

BBC **Shropshire** (www.bbc.co.uk/shropshire) - Samantha Hatton for helping Morris set off, Jim Hawkins for talking to him and Trystan Jones for all his hard work keeping him going.

Paul Mcavoy , Lee Furness, Melvin Bone, Joe Summerfield, James the Shropshire Lad, Mike Batt, Sir Funkalot, M(via Tibberton), Clive Bevan, The Mailman and everyone else who joined in on the Morris Telford BBC message board.

John Richard Whiteley and Carol Vorderman for inspiration and diversion.

And of course, everyone in Shropshire, especially the lucky, lucky people of **Moreton Say**.